Industrial Letchworth

The First Garden City 1903-1920

First published in Great Britain in 2021 by

Hertfordshire Publications
an imprint of
University of Hertfordshire Press
College Lane
Hatfield
Hertfordshire
AL10 9AB

British Library Cataloguing in Publication Data

A catalogue record for this book is available from the British Library

ISBN 978-1-912260-28-7

Design by Helen Nelson, www.jetthedog.co.uk

Printed in Great Britain by Hobbs the Printers Ltd

Garden City
Collection

Front cover: *Workers outside the W. H. Smith & Son bindery c.1910 –12, a building still standing at the junction of Works Road and Pixmore Avenue. A postcard produced for the Garden Cities and Town Planning Association. Digital colourisation by Claudia D'Souza, The Photo Alchemist.*

CONTRIBUTORS AND ACKNOWLEDGEMENTS

This book was written by members of Letchworth Local History Research Group, Letchworth Garden City, Hertfordshire:

Janet Capstick, Mertsi Fisher, John Gregory, Philippa Parker and Anthony Simms, with contributions from Louise Fryer, Alison Gillan, and Stephen Parker and support from Kathy and Bob Culver and Dr Kate Thompson.

Edited by Janet Capstick and Philippa Parker.

We are pleased to acknowledge help received from:

The staff of Letchworth Garden City Heritage Foundation and the Garden City Collection – Victoria Axell, Aimee Flack, Josh Tidy and Sophie Walters; the staff of Hertfordshire Archives and Local Studies; Katy Lock, Town and Country Planning Association, London; Charlotte Harding and Hannah Auerbach George of the Warner Textile Archive, Braintree, Essex; Kim Fisher; Richard Hunter; Sarah Elvins and Jane Housham, University of Hertfordshire Press; Anne Coste, Stéphane Sadoux and Susannah O'Carroll, Grenoble School of Architecture.

This publication was supported by a public grant overseen by the French National Research Agency (ANR) as part of the "Investissements d'Avenir" program (reference: ANR-10-LABX-0078).

Financial support was also received from Letchworth Garden City Heritage Foundation, North Hertfordshire District Council, Letchworth Garden City Society and those local businesses who sponsored the 2015 exhibition about Letchworth's early industrial origins 1905–1920.

Advertising poster promoting Letchworth as a location for speedy transport of goods across the country, c.1910–1913.

Contents

FOREWORD

From The Marquess of Salisbury

The Garden City movement was a British phenomenon that grew out of the ideas Ebenezer Howard, propounded in his 'Garden Cities of To-morrow' in 1902. There was already in this country a well-established habit of building model workers' settlements around paternalistic or idealistic employers' factories: places like Saltaire, Port Sunlight, New Lanark and Bournville. However, these settlements depended on a single employer, on the prosperity of a single enterprise and on the employer's successors sharing his vision.

The garden cities sought to establish more broadly based communities with a mix of employment and a greater self-sufficiency. The countryside had to play a part in the settlements' life, as did the arts and entertainment. Letchworth enjoys a proud position as the first Garden City. It has acted as a model throughout the world and has become a place of pilgrimage for town planners.

The effects on the people from industrial Britain who came to settle in Letchworth were remarkable. Children, for instance, were healthier by far, better educated and more balanced.

This short book is a timely and scholarly achievement.

We live in a rapidly urbanising world and we have a choice: we can allow people to live in new urban slums, or we can build places where people want to live and work and be part of a thriving community. So there is room for our experience of garden cities to contribute to the urgent debate about the various ways we can achieve these objectives.

Equally, we have a shortage of housing in this country and how we satisfy that demand is as important as the raw numbers of houses built. Indeed, Letchworth itself is about to embark on its next phase of expansion, to include housing for all parts of the market.

So it is particularly interesting to have a frank analysis of how the fathers of Letchworth answered the questions that faced them in the first phase of the garden city's development, including the important question of how best to provide affordable housing.

I am proud to have been asked to be associated with Letchworth and look forward not only to the contribution it will continue to make to building its own community, but also to the wider debate on how best we can build communities in a wider world.

Section One

AN INDUSTRIAL UTOPIA

The share certificate form reads:

FIRST GARDEN CITY LIMITED.

No. _____

CAPITAL - - - - - £300,000,

Divided into **59,400** Shares of **£5** each, and **3,000** Shares of **£1** each.

ISSUE OF **32,848** SHARES OF **£5** EACH.

Being balance of **£5** Shares.

FORM OF APPLICATION FOR SHARES.

To the Directors, FIRST GARDEN CITY LIMITED, 326a, High Holborn, London, W.C.

GENTLEMEN,

Having paid to the Company's Bankers the sum of _____, being
(1) payment in full
(2) a deposit of 10s. per Share } on application for _____ Ordinary Shares of **£5** each in the above-named
Company, I hereby request you to allot me that number of Shares, upon the terms of the prospectus of the Company dated the 11th of June, 1906, and I agree to accept the same or any smaller number that may be allotted to me, and I agree to make the remaining payments in respect thereof in accordance with the said Prospectus ; and I authorise you to register me as the holder of the Shares so allotted to me.

Name (in full) _____

NOTE.—
PLEASE WRITE
VERY DISTINCTLY.

Description (Mr. Mrs. or Miss) _____

Address (in full) _____

_____

Occupation _____

Date _____ Signature _____

All Cheques should be made payable to the Bankers of the Company, the London City and Midland Bank Limited.

FIRST GARDEN CITY LIMITED.

BANKER'S RECEIPT FOR APPLICATION.

Received this _____ day of _____ 190__

from _____ the sum of _____

pounds, _____ shillings and _____ pence, being { payment in full / a deposit of 10s. per Share } on

Shares of £5 each in FIRST GARDEN CITY LIMITED.

For the LONDON CITY AND MIDLAND BANK LIMITED.

STAMP. CASHIER.

£ _____ : _____ : _____

NOTE.—After this receipt is returned from the Bankers it must be carefully preserved to be exchanged in due course for Certificate.

(vertical text on left margin) This Form must be sent ENTIRE, together with Cheque for amount payable, to the Company's Bankers, THE LONDON CITY AND MIDLAND BANK Ltd., 100-101, Fore Street, London, E.C.

INTRODUCTION

About the book

This book follows a successful local history exhibition in October 2015 aimed at raising the profile and increasing understanding of the importance of the industrial aspect of the Letchworth (Garden City) story. Focusing on the pioneer years up to and including 1920, it draws on additional research by members of the Letchworth Local History Group (now Letchworth Local History Research Group) and also uses material from the 2015 exhibition. There are many academic books written about Garden Cities as a model for new towns, including the first garden city, but this book has been written by local residents with a passion for local history and Letchworth. It is hoped it proves an engaging and interesting work as well as a useful reference book for a wide audience.

Key to the project has been stitching back together the industrial storyline from fragmented archive material. What has emerged is a need to ensure that the heritage credentials of Letchworth as a garden city are accurately portrayed and understood – as both an industrial and residential town.

The first section of the book covers:

- what First Garden City Ltd (the Company) sought to achieve in building a new town.

- how the Company got started – planning Letchworth, who was involved, the sequence of development and rationale behind this to ensure the success of the industrial aspect (including critical infrastructure).

- how First Garden City Ltd attracted manufacturers, and the wider marketing campaign.

- financing the venture; who were the main shareholders and how did they go about raising the necessary capital?

- where the factory workers lived, cottage building and population growth.

The second part of the book explores some of the pioneer industries which came, providing background about the companies, their employees and experiences at Letchworth.

Letchworth – the experiment

Letchworth (Garden City) was an experiment of significant scale designed to encourage mass movement of manufacturers from crowded industrial centres through the development of a new town in a planned way. First Garden City Ltd took Ebenezer Howard's garden cities model and adapted it, with the central aim of delivering a better quality of life and overall wellbeing for those working and living in the town. It built Letchworth as a model industrial town which was designed to be self-supporting.

Although seeking to deliver public good, Letchworth was a bold commercial venture by First Garden City Ltd (FGC Ltd) and something incredibly unique which would be difficult to repeat today. It differed from other smaller schemes like Bournville, Port Sunlight and Saltaire which were developed to support a single industry. Letchworth was designed to attract diverse manufacturing and industrial firms, and thereby a critical mass of employment for men and women within the town and neighbouring villages on the estate. Such a mix of trades was not accidental but deliberate, to ensure Letchworth would not be reliant on one main sector. Alongside this it was also designed as a pleasant residential town.

The role of the Company

FGC Ltd acted as an enabler, providing key infrastructure and sites for development which it managed in line with a clear development plan and strategy. It was never its intention to undertake large scale building of houses or factories on the estate; instead this was to be left to the market. The Company did have to intervene early on to help facilitate provision of cottages for labourers and workers through the establishment of building and finance companies to contract with, and provide mortgages to, builders and manufacturers to support the residential and industrial aims.

Being the sole landowner meant FGC Ltd also had control over the release and management of sites as development progressed. There was phased release of land (in plots) in order to manage the level of capital outlay necessary for the supporting infrastructure to get sites ready for development. Leasing, rather than selling, plots enabled the Company to retain control and ensure the increase in value of land (as it was developed) could be captured and reinvested for the benefit of the town and its residents.

The industrial achievement

Eighty-two factories and workshops were established in the industrial areas of the new garden city between 1905 and 1920. The timeline published with this book includes the most significant of the industrial pioneers, together with a number of smaller firms, to demonstrate the diversity of Letchworth's industrial base. Among these were established firms developing additional facilities, brand new enterprises and relocations. Companies were attracted from towns and cities across the country and some from overseas, although over half either moved works from London or extended operations by building additional facilities in Letchworth. Not all were successful once established at Letchworth – some did flourish, some floundered and others simply moved on. Many of the manufacturers were attracted for very practical business reasons but some were also specifically attracted by the garden city ideals and wanted to be part of this wonderful experiment. Interestingly, some of the more sceptical industrialists were also converts following positive experiences at Letchworth.

The advent of the First World War could have completely derailed the scheme. Remember, Letchworth (Garden City) was still relatively new by 1914 and even though the war impacted on the pace of development, the town retained most of the larger pioneer industries and attracted new firms. This shows that within eleven years this relatively new town had reached a critical mass which not only withstood the impact of the war but also adapted and flourished during the most testing of times. Many existing industries had turned over to munitions work. Kryn & Lahy, who became one of Letchworth's largest engineering firms, was established for war work in 1915.

Letchworth owes much to its pioneering industrialists who either had faith in the vision of the Garden City Association and belief that the Directors of the First Garden City Company would deliver the facilities necessary to support industry or were prepared to take a risk. Without them, Letchworth would not have become such a successful and thriving industrial and residential town.

With Letchworth, Directors of First Garden City Ltd provided a viable garden city example on a scale not seen before. The importance of Letchworth's rich industrial and manufacturing heart to its overall success cannot be underestimated. It not only provided a solid economic base but also the foundation for a diverse and inclusive town with all the facilities needed for a self-sufficient place. The sense of community spirit and pride in Letchworth at the time was significant. Letchworth represented new beginnings, hope and opportunity. Industry was central to the garden city model pursued by First Garden City Ltd, Letchworth's founders.

A unique example

For the future it is important Letchworth can retain a diverse industrial heart, accepting it must evolve with the times to remain relevant and sustainable. This book underlines why Letchworth is such a unique example as the world's first garden city and every effort must be made to protect and enhance the industrial/residential balance (in line with the needs of the town today). Unfortunately, at the time of writing this book its future is under threat from the demands of housing growth and weakening of its industrial base. It is sincerely hoped that the planning system which Letchworth helped shape does not turn into the very thing that ruins this wonderful garden city.

FIRST GARDEN CITY LTD AND THEIR MODEL TOWN

A collaborative achievement

Letchworth's development was led by First Garden City Ltd and owed its success to the many individuals associated with the work of the Company. Yet it is predominantly Ebenezer Howard and the architects – Barry Parker and Raymond Unwin – who are remembered and celebrated. It is so important, too, to recognise and not forget the contributions of others, including:

- *Skilled surveyors and engineers* – without their input the architects and the Company could not have developed the right kind of plan for Letchworth, including the critical infrastructure needed for the industries and the town.

- *Company secretaries and estate managers* – who led the practical delivery of the scheme and helped promote Letchworth and supported the FGC Ltd Board.

- *Company chairmen and directors* – who worked tirelessly to realise the vision, find the necessary capital to deliver and who didn't shy away from significant challenges through the early years.

- *Wider shareholders and supporters* – willing to risk their money and provide support and time for the cause. These were some very influential individuals who went above and beyond the call of duty at times, providing additional lending and persuading others of the value of the cause.

- *The hundreds of unemployed men from London* – who provided much needed labour to complete the initial infrastructure and help out with other early construction projects.

- *Ordinary citizens* – who moved their lives to Letchworth, either because they had to – following their employer – or because they wanted to be part of this new and exciting place.

- *Pioneer industrialists* – without whom this model industrial and residential town may well have faltered.

This book celebrates the collaborative effort which underpinned such an important social experiment. It also identifies some of the key challenges which were faced as the industries arrived and the town rapidly grew. Although the industrial aspect was key to Letchworth's success, the Company released residential plots first. Doing this meant that they could secure immediate rental income without such a large capital outlay on infrastructure. The factory sites were released once the necessary infrastructure was in place and this early emphasis on

Ralph Neville
(Chairman between
1903–1906)

Aneurin Williams
(Chairman between
1906–1915)

John E Champney
(Chairman between
1915–1920).
Source: Art UK

Henry Blackwall
Harris (Chairman
between 1920–1929)

residential letting may explain why the industrial aspect is less well appreciated within the town's heritage.

The central role of strong leadership throughout the first decades

Financing the development of the estate, particularly in the first decade, was a significant challenge and many accounts of Letchworth write of considerable difficulties. It was vital to have enough capital available to maintain the momentum of development. Company accounts, however, show Directors were able to find solutions to secure financing. An AGM Report from December 1920 refers to then Chairman Henry Blackwell Harris reflecting on the significant contributions of each of the Chairmen up to that date. He said *"At each crucial period of our career the right Chairman seems to have been given us."* Reflecting on individuals Harris said:

- Ralph Neville (Chairman between 1903 and 1906) – he was remembered for his *"energy, organising ability and directness of character [to which] so large a measure of our success has been due".*

- Aneurin Williams (Chairman between 1906 and 1915) was *"known as the conjuror for he produced money as though it were from the air".* Harris went on to talk of Williams' sustained enthusiasm as well as the large amount of money he put into the Company, which Harris felt encouraged others.

- John E Champney (Chairman between 1915 and 1920) took the helm on behalf of Harris (who was away on military service) and Champney *"… with his sound and wide business advice steered us very safely through the very difficult period of the war, owing to which the new ground rents created fell from £532 in 1913 to £7 in 1917".*

Without the strength of leadership provided by the Company Chairmen and Directors, Letchworth may very well have floundered.

Was the scale of demand for workers' housing underestimated?

Once a body of industry had been established, being able to provide enough accommodation for all the workers was a continuing challenge for the Company. Remember, much of the early house building was for more affluent individuals, including Company shareholders, not labourers and factory workers. Did the Company not anticipate this being a real problem? Was it simply an oversight with everything else going on and were they really caught out? The sequence of development, financing the garden city and the housing challenge is explored later in this first section.

More than a town built on a book

There is an important distinction between Letchworth Garden City's creator, First Garden City Ltd, and Ebenezer Howard. The town is the outcome of the work of the Company with which Ebenezer Howard (as Managing Director) was closely involved.

This is a significant point as the first injustice to the legacy of First Garden City Ltd is blithely to refer to Letchworth as a "town built on a book". The town is not a replica of Ebenezer's scheme but a practical experiment which took the ideas in his book – *Garden Cities of To-morrow* (1902) – and modified them as necessary to deliver a commercially viable scheme which suited the land purchased.

One of Letchworth's founders, Ralph Neville, KC, (Chair of the Garden City Association, Garden City Pioneer Company and later First Garden City) spoke in 1904 of the garden city model as a method of industrial redistribution. This speech was given at a time when Neville and his Company Directors were still finalising the finer details of the purchase of the Letchworth estate and the architects and engineers were working on a viable plan. Ralph Neville acknowledged that the Garden City project was the outcome of Ebenezer Howard's ideas and that interest in this had led to the formation of the Garden City Association, which had the aim of taking the garden city idea and putting it into practice.

In order to do this and also continue to further the garden cities' cause, the Association set up a scheme-specific commercial entity. Those involved in the Garden City Association at the time described it as consisting of two bodies – the Association being the educational body and the Company (first the Pioneer Company and then First Garden City) the practical body. Many of the Association's shareholders also invested in the Companies.

The Garden City Association itself was focused on spreading the word, garnering support and investment for the movement and influencing other like-minded schemes. The first edition of their journal was published on 1 October 1904 (almost a year after the opening of the Letchworth estate) and an advertisement for that edition stated it was to be a quarterly magazine *"devoted to housing reform and industrial betterment"*. The Garden City Pioneer Company Ltd and then First Garden City Ltd were commercial entities and the practical face of the experiment which took place at Letchworth.

Today we no longer have such a direct connection between these two bodies. The Garden City Association became the Town and Country Planning Association and First Garden City Ltd no longer exists as a commercial entity. The estate which makes up Letchworth Garden City is today under the guardianship of Letchworth Garden City Heritage Foundation, a charitable organisation, who as landlords look after the garden city estate and use income generated from their property portfolio to invest back into the town.

Misunderstanding and misrepresentation

Across numerous press articles, reports of lectures, and discussions of the time there is evidence of misrepresentation and misunderstandings of what constituted a "garden city" and exactly what was happening at Letchworth. Representatives of the Company and the Association sought to correct this wherever possible in their publicity material, letters to the press, speeches and the Association's own journal articles. While the Association was keen to support and promote the model, many smaller schemes incorrectly tried to claim a garden city label.

An interesting article published in the Association's quarterly journal in February 1915, commenting on the success of Letchworth, had this to say on the matter (this was before Welwyn Garden City):

There can be no doubt that Letchworth would receive far wider and more substantial support if it were realised that Mr. Howard's magnificent experiment constitutes not only the first but the only garden city in existence in this country. Admirable suburban developments on "garden city" lines are taking place on every side, but it is difficult to make the public understand that such developments, however welcome, are not garden cities. They are in general beautifully planned and they follow the Letchworth ideal by making ample provision for gardens and open-spaces, but there are many vital distinctions between such developments as these and a self-contained town with its residential quarters, its industrial area, and its great belt of agricultural land. Letchworth draws its population largely from congested urban districts, puts them down right in the heart of the country and enables them to live a fuller, healthier and happier life than is possible in any other town in these kingdoms. It is among the chief aims of the Garden Cities and Town Planning

Association to dissipate the confusion prevailing in the popular mind as to the real meaning of First Garden City and to make it known that only under such conditions as are found at Letchworth can Mr. Howard's famous design be carried out in its entirety.

Even the first sentence in this article muddies the water somewhat given what Ralph Neville wrote in a professional journal in February 1904 (when work was underway on building Letchworth) about the distinction between Ebenezer Howard's idea and what First Garden City wanted to achieve with Letchworth:

… it is necessary to state clearly the extent to which the company are indebted to Mr. Howard, and how far their undertaking is affected by the views stated in his book.

To Mr. Howard belongs the merit of directing public attention to the desirability and possibility of making provision for the increase and overflow of the industrial population by:

1) *Acquiring sites for industrial settlements at agricultural prices*

2) *Scientific planning of the sites by experts*

3) *Concerted migration of population*

4) *Limiting the area and population of these settlements*

5) *Maintaining a belt of agricultural land around them*

6) *Applying the increment in the value of the land for the benefit of the population*

Here begins and ends the connection between Mr. Howard's book and the undertaking of the First Garden City Limited. Mr. Howard provided his central idea with an attractive setting; with this the company has no concern. Some of this may prove capable of realisation; some of it is very possibly fanciful, but the whole of it was expressly stated by him to be suggestive merely, and in his book he expressly says the final and actual scheme will be the outcome of many minds.

Ralph Neville went on to explain the purpose of First Garden City Ltd as

… to proceed with the development of the estate in accordance with the best expert advice they can obtain, having regard to the objects enumerated above. This is the attitude of the directors to-day. This has been the attitude of those engaged in the movement ever since I have been connected with it, and to the best of my belief it was the same from the very inception of the movement.

Now some of the advantages which may be expected to accrue from industrial settlements so organised are:

1) *Conditions of life for the artisan and townsman consistent with sound health for himself, his wife, and his children.*

2) *Cheapness, efficiency and sightliness resulting from the scientific laying out of the town as a whole from the outset. In connection with this head may be grouped:*

a. *The supply of light, water, power and heat*

b. *Facility of transit and communication*

c. *Disposal of sewage*

3) *The reduction of rates, by the application of the increment in the value of the lands, so far as it can be secured for the benefit of the inhabitants*

4) *Bringing a market to the farmers of the agricultural land, and incidentally:*

a. *Increasing the amount of small culture*

b. *Affording the agricultural labourer, the advantages of town life*

Ralph Neville described First Garden City Ltd's undertaking as promoting the decentralisation of industry. Ebenezer Howard also said that the industrial element was an essential part of a garden city. So at least there was synergy around the industrial aspect in all this!

Letchworth the experiment and model town

Letchworth's founders and those involved more broadly in the garden city movement agreed that to deal properly with the problems of overcrowding in existing cities and towns and also the depopulation of rural districts the only solution would be to build a new town from scratch.

The strength of feeling about this is captured perfectly in the prospectus from the registration of First Garden City Ltd, dated 8 September 1903, which states:

> *The difficulties of dealing with the housing question in our overcrowded industrial centres become increasingly apparent with every fresh attempt at amendment. The expense is enormous, while improvement in one direction frequently increases the evil in another. The only satisfactory way out of the difficulty is to start afresh and establish a new town to which those manufacturers whose businesses admit of such removal may go.*

As this was the first time it had been attempted on such a scale this is perhaps why they often referred to Letchworth as a "great social experiment" which they believed to be of "national importance". Both of these were used in publicity material either promoting the new industrial town or the town's residential credentials.

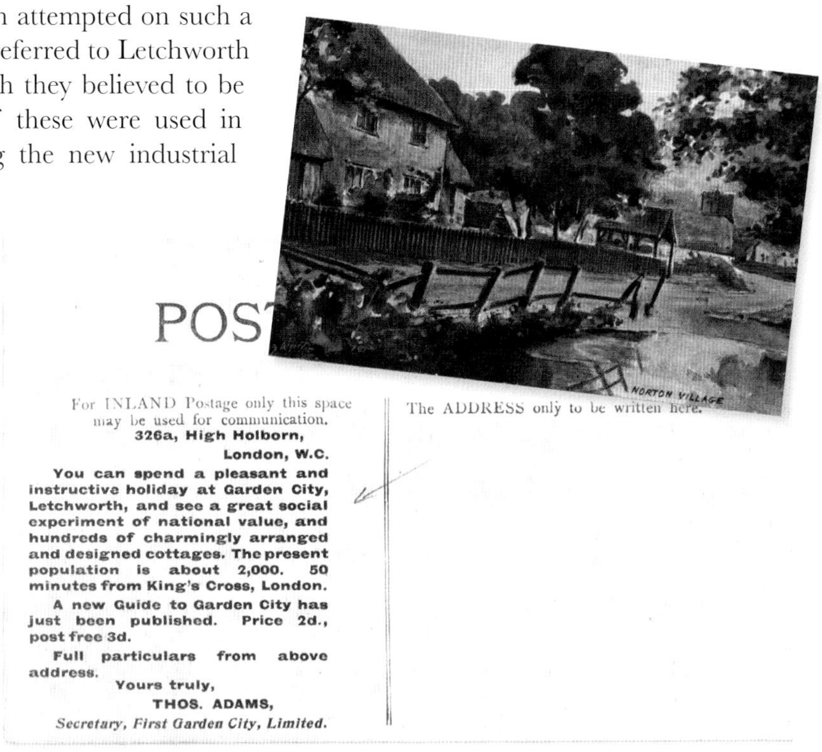
NORTON VILLAGE
POS
For INLAND Postage only this space may be used for communication.
326a, High Holborn, London, W.C.
You can spend a pleasant and instructive holiday at Garden City, Letchworth, and see a great social experiment of national value, and hundreds of charmingly arranged and designed cottages. The present population is about 2,000. 50 minutes from King's Cross, London.
A new Guide to Garden City has just been published. Price 2d., post free 3d.
Full particulars from above address.
Yours truly,
THOS. ADAMS,
Secretary, First Garden City, Limited.
The ADDRESS only to be written here.

One of a series of local postcards featuring paintings by the artist Louis Weirter (Thomas Adams' brother-in-law); used by First Garden City Ltd for marketing purposes.

The Directors of First Garden City Ltd hoped to build on the success of other smaller schemes built around a single employer, particularly those at Port Sunlight and Bournville, and wholeheartedly believed that their garden city model of developing a brand new industrial town would deliver a solution. In their 1903 prospectus the Directors also stated it could "… *maintain and increase industrial efficiency without impairing the national physique*". The health of the industrial workforce at the time was a particular concern and poor working and living conditions were exacerbating this. So, definitely the scale and method of what took place at Letchworth are what distinguishes it from other smaller but equally well-meaning schemes.

W H Lever and the Cadburys were amongst the highly influential industrial advocates of the scheme, especially Edward Cadbury, himself also a Director of the Company between 1903 and 1919. FGC Ltd also borrowed money on mortgage from the Bournville Works Pension Fund, contributing much needed capital for progressing development. Lever resigned as a Director in spring 1904 but remained a shareholder.

At the Letchworth estate opening on 9 October 1903, Earl Grey (not only a figurehead but also a shareholder and supporter of the movement) spoke of his initial scepticism about the deliverability of such an ambitious utopia but also said he was by then a total convert. Although this was still early days for Letchworth a huge amount of work had already been done by all those involved. It was widely reported that another dignitary present at the opening ceremony for the estate, Viscount Peel, *"… welcomed the experiment by First Garden City to build a model industrial town."*

So, it is clear from Company publications, records and reports of the time that Letchworth was intended and promoted as both an industrial and residential town. It was viewed very much as a model town with the twin aims of delivering both improved working and living conditions. First Garden City Ltd set out to develop a mixed town which appealed to manufacturers, workers and artisans alike. The other key point was, of course, that it was to be properly planned to avoid the mistakes of the past and this is where the skills of the surveyors and engineers as well as the architects were key.

Industry – the golden thread

The industrial story of Letchworth Garden City starts with the creation of the Garden City Association in terms of awareness-raising, garnering support and fact finding and then continues apace with the formation of the Garden City Pioneer Company Ltd and then First Garden City Ltd. The need to encourage movement of manufacturers was a thread which ran through all considerations for the new town, from the site search and selection through to the planning and location of critical infrastructure and the siting of the industrial quarter.

The Garden City Association, through its lectures, conferences, visits and members, actively promoted the cause and sought interested investors and manufacturers from the start. Press reports of the Association's activities show key advocates of the time – Ebenezer Howard, Ralph Neville and Thomas Adams – travelling the length and breadth of the country attending and giving lectures. Others, including W H Lever and George Cadbury, provided support, for example by hosting and attending events organised and promoted by the Association. In June 1902 a public meeting was organised in Holborn, London (where the Association had its offices):

> to consider how far overcrowding and congestion in large cities can be overcome by concerted movement of manufacturers, co-operators and others to new areas on which arrangements will be made for securing to the migrating people the whole of the increased value to which their presence would give the sites.

Ebenezer Howard, Thomas Adams, Ralph Neville, Aneurin Williams, Thomas Ritzema (a well-known newspaper magnate and shareholder), Walter Crane and W H Lever were all present and involved in the proceedings. Walter Crane reportedly even designed souvenir tickets for the event. Looking at the archive material available, it is clear that events organised by the Association and its associated companies were well planned, publicised and targeted for maximum impact. As early as December 1902, and parallel with the site search work that culminated in the selection of the estate at Hitchin for Letchworth, the Garden City Pioneer Company was actively canvassing manufacturers (this initial company was established solely to find and purchase a suitable site). They targeted individual manufacturers, writing about the search for a site and seeking interest in moving works or expanding to a new garden city site. This turned into a concerted and ultimately successful campaign which was continued mainly via First Garden City Ltd but also the Garden City Association.

Initial emphasis was on publicising the venture and seeking expressions of interest as the Directors knew that any significant movement of manufacturers could only take place once the necessary conditions were in place. A conference for manufacturers was held, taking place on 1 April 1903 at the Pioneer Company offices. Although this is recorded as an important event it has not been possible to find the record of the proceedings held in the Garden City Collection. It is, however, mentioned in Mervyn Miller's book on Letchworth; it was clearly a working conference to find out what the key considerations were for manufacturers and where and how they could be persuaded to move.

More evidence of the manufacturers and industrialists who eventually came to Letchworth can be traced in very early correspondence, press cuttings and other documents from the Pioneer Company days. Bert Williams, who founded the Garden City Press as a co-operative printing enterprise, was an active supporter of the Association and the co-operative movement overall and often involved in events and conferences. He came to Letchworth from Leicester to establish a co-operative print works at the garden city and was part of the wider Letchworth co-operative movement. Such was his belief in the cause that he even set up temporary works in Hitchin at the end of 1903 until it was possible to develop a site at Letchworth. Garden City Press went on to become a long-standing employer in the town although not a co-operative enterprise much beyond its early years. Bert Williams took a remarkable leap of faith at a time when Letchworth was predominately agricultural land, certainly no sign of the town it was to become. George Ewart of Ewart and Sons, engineers, was another manufacturer keen to expand his enterprise into Letchworth. Ewart's son – George Herbert Ewart – even visited potential sites being considered by the Pioneer Company. Ewart senior wrote to Ebenezer Howard upon hearing that the Pioneer Company had agreed on a site for the new garden city. But, even though Ewart was the first manufacturer to sign a lease (in June 1904), they didn't actually develop their site until much later, with the factory finally operational some six years after. Thomas Howell Idris, a shareholder and director, expanded his existing operations in Camden, London, by opening a bottling plant for his Idris mineral waters in Letchworth, building a new factory in Glebe Road.

London County Tram (Stamford Hill route) c.1909, advertising land and factory sites available at Letchworth.

Archive, publicity, and marketing material published by FGC Ltd show a definite twin track approach, promoting the industrial or residential aspects of the scheme, depending on the target audience. The Garden City Collection has many examples of the early publicity used.

These include industrial promotional pamphlets, postcards, train timetables, programmes for organised set piece visits or opening ceremonies, which were geared towards showcasing the various aspects of the town and its benefits over other crowded areas.

The Company also took part in many exhibitions up and down the country, including the great Franco-British Exhibition at White City between May and October 1908. They also paid for a series of posters on London County trams, including promotion on tram tickets and timetables during 1909. One striking

image shows one of these trams advertising factory sites to let at Letchworth. Company accounts provide evidence of such special advertising and exhibitions undertaken, as well as the usual publicity and advertising in periodicals of the time. An entry in the FGC Ltd accounts for 1909 – Special Advertising and Exhibitions – under the costs for their stand at the Electrical Exhibition at Manchester shows a charge of £4 8s for supplying four signs: "There is no place like Letchworth". This is the same year the Company exhibited at the Franco-British, Earls Court and Edinburgh Exhibitions.

DEVELOPING THE LAND AT HITCHIN WAS A RISK

Thomas Adams c.1903, (Secretary and Estate Manager for First Garden City Ltd 1903–1906)

Harold Craske (Company Secretary First Garden City Ltd 1906–1939)

William H Gaunt (Estate Manager, First Garden City Ltd 1905–1917)

Mervyn Miller's book on Letchworth *(Letchworth: The First Garden City)* covers the site search and selection process in detail so this is not repeated in this book. Led by the Garden City Pioneer Company it understandably occupied many months. It has been suggested previously that this process was chaotic and Miller's book quotes Charles B Purdom's reporting of growing confusion at the Pioneer Company during the site search process.

However, early Pioneer Company correspondence records contradict this, so perhaps it was not as chaotic as it may have seemed to Purdom. He was, after all, at the time a junior clerk at the Garden City Association so it is unlikely he would have had access to all the facts. There is, however, no doubt that the Pioneer Company received lots of information about many estates for sale but its Directors were well advised and clear about what was needed. Archive records verify this and that the process was extensive and well scrutinised. This ensured the land purchased for development would be capable of supporting a new town and within that able to provide the facilities necessary for manufacturers as economically as possible. For example, some of the consulting engineers who worked with First Garden City Ltd on infrastructure and utilities were also involved in assessing the merits or otherwise of estates seriously considered (e.g. Howard Humphreys and G R Strachan).

Interested manufacturers (e.g. George H Ewart), including Board members, also visited shortlisted sites, with Board members particularly needing to ensure they were well informed to vote on the best option. This all points to a thorough process and one ably managed by Thomas Adams who was, successively, Secretary of the Garden City Association, the Garden City Pioneer Company and then First Garden City Ltd until he left the Company in November 1906.

By February 1903 three estates had been shortlisted – Chartley Castle, Staffordshire, Grendon Estate, near Atherston, Warwickshire, and Crouch Estate in Essex. They were assessed at a Pioneer Company Board meeting on 26 February 1903 and by late April 1903 the Company had a three-month option to purchase the Chartley Castle estate. This got as far as commissioning a valuation, which didn't proceed, as by May 1903 favourable views started to be expressed about land near Hitchin. The Company's water engineer, G R Strachan, advised that the water supply on that land was much more satisfactory than at Chartley; other advantages included proximity to London, which would, amongst other things, give it a high value for residential purposes (how true!). Let us not forget that the earlier conference for manufacturers had provided valuable insight into the importance of location and other key considerations for firms. The fact that there was a ready supply of labour at Hitchin and Baldock weighed highly too. The Pioneer Company decided at its Board meeting on 28 May 1903 to obtain options on the land near Hitchin.

Even when this land was under consideration it is clear certain Board members, including Ebenezer Howard, were nervous about making any rash decisions. He wrote to the Chartley agents in mid-June 1903 asking that the option for purchasing remain open. It is easy to understand his concerns as pursuing the land at Hitchin was a big risk. The scheme needed a significant area secured within a ring fence so, for the land at Hitchin to be suitable, the Company had to purchase thirteen adjoining, but separate, parcels of land held by 15 different owners; not completing on any one of these would have rendered the scheme a non-starter.

Thomas Adams and Letchworth

First Garden City exhibition stand promoting Letchworth at the Franco-British Exhibition, White City, 1908.

Although Thomas Adams' time at Letchworth was relatively brief, he remains an important contributor to its success. As Company Secretary he visited every estate which was considered by the Pioneer Company, advising Board members, and ultimately played a lead role in the site search and selection process and the decision to choose the land near Hitchin on which Letchworth was developed.

In the early days of development the role of Company Secretary for FGC Ltd must have been extremely demanding for Thomas Adams and his successor, Harold Craske. Added to that, Adams was also Estate Manager (prior to the appointment of William Gaunt) for two years, alongside his role as Secretary. This meant he would have been busy dealing with enquiries from prospective tenants, day-to-day estate matters, as well as supporting the Board with promotion and securing the finance for the venture. On top of all this Adams identified the opportunity and secured the holding of the 1905 Cheap Cottages Exhibition at Letchworth. This delivered massive publicity, tens of thousands of visitors and much needed cottages in the first year of significant developments. He was very active and involved across all fronts of Company business and well respected by Directors. In an article on his resignation which featured in the *The Garden City* journal of September 1906 he is recognised as *"... having secured and carried through all negotiations with all Manufacturers ..."* At that time there were twelve factories operating or in the course of construction and it is these pioneer industries which helped persuade those that followed, underlining again the importance of Adams' achievements. Visiting Letchworth in 1932, Adams recalled that in Letchworth's early days he had spent a great deal of his life blood for First Garden City. It is easy to appreciate quite why!

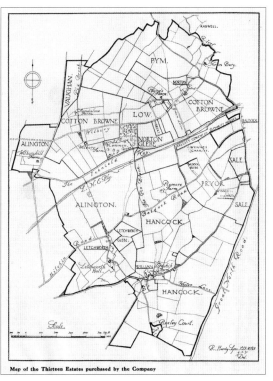

Map of the Thirteen Estates purchased by the Company

Map of the 13 estates purchased by the Company to complete the scheme.

LANDHOLDING, AGRICULTURE, AND SMALLHOLDING

Landholding, agriculture and smallholding in the early years of Letchworth Garden City

Hertfordshire at the end of the nineteenth century was a mainly agricultural county of farmland, small woods, a network of minor lowland rivers and a large number of privately owned parks and small estates of 800–1,000 acres. Apart from a few major landowners, these were held by the newly wealthy who had made their money in trade, business and the professions. The geology of north Hertfordshire is chalk overlain by clay, generally well drained, regarded at the time as an indicator of a healthy environment. Within the dominant industry of agriculture the main arable crops were malting barley for making beer and wheat for flour. A by-product of the latter was wheat straw for the cottage industry of straw plaiting, which became established around 1800 when straw bonnets for women became fashionable. This was the terrain on which the first garden city was built and the nature of the all-important agricultural belt around it.

Letchworth's site had eventually been chosen over others because of its proximity to London, an existing railway line, level land with an ample water supply and the relatively low cost of the thirteen individual landholdings which were stitched together to form the estate. First Garden City Ltd bought 3,818 acres of land at £40 15s an acre. The price was low because of the poor quality of the soil (improved somewhat by the spreading of manure from London brought by train) and because by 1903 agriculture in England was enduring a period of depression.

In the 1850s and 1860s (after the repeal of the Corn Laws in 1846) agriculture flourished, helped by scientific advances such as field drainage and new fertilisers. However, from the 1870s onwards (in fact until the Second World War) agriculture as an industry was depressed. The causes were several. The end of the American Civil War in 1865 led to settlement across the prairies and the building of trans-continental railroads. Commodity prices fell as cheap wheat from the large farms of North America was imported into Europe by fast steam ships. Techniques for chilling and freezing meat enabled cheap supplies from Australasia and Argentina. There was a series of poor summers in the 1870s, transport costs in England rose, nouveau riche landlords were often absent from their farms and neglectful of their upkeep and the tradition of annual tenancies did not encourage tenant farmers to invest in farm buildings or equipment.

A typical Letchworth smallholding

14

Arable counties like Hertfordshire were badly affected by these circumstances. The value of land for agriculture dropped and estates were instead marketed for their residential or sporting potential, with emphasis on the convenience and health of life in the county. Hertfordshire was poised to become an urbanised county of commuters.

Workers had begun leaving the land before the agricultural recession for a number of reasons. Rural society was limited and the growing railway network enabled greater mobility. Agricultural wages and work opportunities were falling behind those available in towns, especially for those with skills, for example, a man who could handle horses. A policeman, postman, road mender or railway navvy could earn more than a farm worker (whose average weekly wage in 1906 was 14s 11d) and employment was more secure all the year round. Although the population was rising, fewer workers were needed as machinery replaced humans and the products of manufacture could pay for cheap foreign food.

Rural industries such as straw plaiting, which had mainly been done by women and children to supplement the family income, also faced competition from cheaper imports from the Far East. In the nineteenth century 60 per cent of adult males worked on the land, 45 per cent as agricultural labourers, almost always on land owned by someone else. Labourers were hired by the week or even the day and lived in rented cottages. By 1900 there was a severe shortage of accommodation for rural dwellers as building by-laws combined with low rents made it uneconomic for landlords to build or even repair cottages. Towns like Hitchin were becoming overcrowded and insanitary because of this lack of housing in the villages. Ironically, it was the economic decline of the countryside, low land values and the fact that new landowners who had little sentimental attachment to their estates were willing to sell that both precipitated and enabled the establishment of the first garden city.

The Pioneer Company's ideas for a garden city

Ebenezer Howard's objectives for a garden city encompassed the halting of rural depopulation by promoting a rural economy and alleviating overcrowding in towns. The first prospectus of the Garden City Pioneer Company announced *"the provision of a broad belt of agricultural land around the town…the combined advantage of town and country…"*. A range of agricultural enterprises was envisaged, from farms to allotments. It was intended that a garden city would be self-sufficient in its food supply and that the town would be a market for rural produce. However, unlike the Company's schemes for attracting industries to Letchworth, there was no overarching development plan for agriculture and little overt advertising. Land reform – a concern of many at the time – was merely a by-product of designing a new town. It may be noted that the early Directors of First Garden City were mostly industrialists and businessmen.

It was Thomas Adams, the Company's Secretary, (who had grown up on his family's Scottish farm) who realised that he had not only to allay local rural concerns about the coming of a town but also to ensure that agricultural policy was not neglected. In September 1904 the Company hosted a conference on *"Garden City and agriculture"* chaired by Henry Rider Haggard, the well-known novelist but also Norfolk landowner and land reformer and a Vice President of the Garden City Association. He was joined by other prominent members of the Land Nationalisation Society (founded in 1892), one of whose campaigns was the promotion of smallholdings to give labourers a personal stake in the land.

The Company saw the need for co-operative purchasing and marketing schemes, cheap loans for smallholders and a concentration on high-value crops and on dairying. It hoped to set up a demonstration farm, an agricultural-research centre, a fruit-tree nursery and village industries to employ workers' families. Alas, very little of this came about. First Garden City's dire lack of capital put paid to these worthy schemes and tenants found the soil of north Hertfordshire (unlike that of neighbouring Bedfordshire) unsuited to market gardening. Many applied to take on a smallholding of between five and twenty acres but then could not afford to build their own cottage on the plot as required by the Company. By 1913 about 300 acres of Letchworth's estate were being cultivated, supporting, in part, a population of around 8,000. Eventually, though, many smallholders found more secure employment in the town's expanding industries.

In the end the Company focused on its industrial and urban policies and only managed to establish one main agricultural enterprise, a 152-acre smallholding centre at Norton Hall Farm. Here the Co-operative Small Holdings Society set up a demonstration and training centre, sub-letting units of up to 25 acres on long leases, and building some cottages. After Thomas Adams left the Company in 1906 his successor as Estate Manager, Walter H Gaunt, gave agriculture even less priority.

First Garden City Ltd did have some success in supporting the rural economy by such works as draining land, building roads and laying hedges. In addition, some industries related to agriculture came to the town. In 1910 the Country Gentleman's Association – an organisation which provided advice to landowners and estates and sold equipment and supplies – moved to Letchworth. They maintained a seed-testing ground on Icknield Way. The Pioneer Nursery was set up on a smallholding at Willian in 1904 by William Tagg and two partners. In 1956 he wrote his account of those early years, claiming *"We were not received very kindly by the surrounding population. They looked on us as interlopers and cranks…and gave us a very short life."* Gradually, First Garden City Ltd saw the wisdom of encouraging dairy farming, to which the land was more suited, and a number of dairies came into being (five by 1907). In 1925, the Company built a model abattoir for use by local livestock farmers.

Early days on the Estate

When First Garden City Ltd bought the Letchworth estate in 1903 it amounted to 3,818 acres of mostly arable land, much of it neglected, with about 400 inhabitants in the three villages of Letchworth, Norton and Willian. In 1912, an additional 750 acres at Willian and Great Wymondley were bought for farmland and housing. Over the years the original farm tenancies were reorganised into sixteen medium-sized farms, 36 smallholdings and twelve acres of allotments. In any case, the Allotments Acts of 1887 and 1890 required local authorities to make available allotments for local people. Many people were employed outside their village. The fifteen agricultural tenancies ranged from two to 841 acres at a time when about twenty per cent of Hertfordshire farms were unoccupied.

The first prospectus issued by First Garden City Ltd, in September 1903, stated its aims as including *"The stimulation of agriculture by bringing a market to the farmer's door"* and *"The relief of the tedium of agricultural life by accessibility to a large town"*. Inevitably, however, some of the original village dwellers were displaced. Once the estate had been purchased, existing tenants were given notice to quit and new tenancy agreements were negotiated. Lack of Company capital meant that it was unable to invest in agricultural infrastructure to any extent and smallholders were expected to be self-supporting and have the means to build their own dwelling. In due course, the farms came to be managed in the conventional way and the city never supplied all its own food needs. There was an enduring risk that the agricultural estate became simply a land bank for urban expansion. As we know, agriculture in the United Kingdom to the present day has needed government subsidy to be viable.

Letchworth's first residents arrived in July 1904 and quickly established a number of agriculturally related businesses. The local Directory for 1907 lists nurserymen, florists, smallholders, seedsmen, farmers and dairymen. The Letchworth Horticultural Society held its first show in August 1906 and J. M. Dent and W. H. Smith & Son employees started gardening clubs. In truth, whilst the retail provision of the early town remained limited, many families relied on the food they could grow for themselves. One of these pioneers was W G "Bill" Furmston who brought his family from London to a two-acre smallholding on Baldock Road. The adjoining quarter acre was for him to build a dwelling for which he was able to raise a mortgage from the Co-operative Building Society. He planted many fruit trees and employed a labourer to help manage the plot. Furmston concluded that although he had been able to feed his large family and enjoy cultivating his piece of land, he rarely did more than break even. Like other smallholders, he did not have enough spare capital to expand his farming activities and neither did First Garden City have funds to subsidise these early smallholders.

Pioneer residents, the family of William Furmston, later landlord of The Skittles Inn.

Although most of First Garden City's plans for the revitalisation of agriculture in and around Letchworth either went unrealised or faded away – because of chronic lack of investment, changing agricultural practices and social movement – perhaps the most enduring and valuable legacy of those early days is the Green Belt of land which we can but hope will continue to surround the First Garden City.

Milk delivery by a woman from Letchworh Hall Farm.

FINANCING THE FIRST GARDEN CITY

We can date Letchworth Garden City's official beginning to 9 October 1903. On that day Earl Grey – former Liberal MP and Chairman of the Letchworth Pioneer Company – declared the estate open. In incessant rain, speeches were given to a gathering of a thousand visitors and tours of the site made. Before this could happen, however, there had been several years of campaigning and fundraising by those who had been inspired by the writing and oratory of Ebenezer Howard and others.

In June 1899 the Garden City Association had been established, taking its place alongside groups such as the Land Nationalisation Society, whose chairman was Ralph Neville KC, another former Liberal MP. By October of that year, as quoted in Beevers' biography, Howard had claimed that *"The Association numbers among its members manufacturers, co-operators, architects, artists, medical men, financial experts, lawyers, merchants, ministers of religion, members of the London County Council (Moderate and Progressive), socialists and individualists, Radicals and Conservatives."* This set the pattern for the promotion and financing of the First Garden City; its supporters were also its investors and were mainly the "great and the good" of their day, people who were acquainted with each other socially and professionally. By 1902 thee Association had over 1300 members, including 101 "Vice-Presidents"; these included figures such as George Cadbury, Joseph Rowntree, Cecil Harmsworth and H.G. Wells. These leading members were influential in society and with the Press but, crucially, were able to invest in the new venture.

Share certificate for the Garden City Pioneer Company Ltd.

In turn, the Garden City Association set up the Garden City Pioneer Company in June 1902 (with a working capital of £20,000) to find and acquire a site for a garden city. Various sites across England were considered but the Company's Secretary Herbert Warren championed Letchworth because of its proximity to London. Indeed, manufacturers from the capital were seeking sites for expansion outside the metropolis. Its prospectus was widely advertised in newspapers (sometimes at no charge because the proprietors supported the cause) and the share issue was fully subscribed before the end of the year. The Pioneer Company directors were well known figures who invested their own money and this may have given a false sense of the ease of the task ahead. Nevertheless, the Pioneer Company found and bought thirteen separate parcels of land for £155,587 (at an average cost of £40 per acre) as the site for Letchworth Garden City. Its job done, it was wound up and First Garden City Ltd was registered on 1 September 1903, with a share capital of £300,000. Its Board of Directors were mostly those of the Pioneer Company, with the addition of William H Lever, but Ebenezer Howard himself had to be given £100 by the Pioneer Company to pay for his qualifying shares as a Director of FGC. Apart from Howard (who had no other income), no director was paid a salary or fees for his work on behalf of the Company until 1920. Although by 1903 women were participating in public life on a wide range of boards and committees and many were Letchworth shareholders, none was on the Board of Directors nor the Parish Council of 1908. It was not until the formation of the Urban District Council in 1919 that three women were elected to that body. The first company prospectus was issued on 8 September 1903 and the hard work of raising capital could begin.

The first company directors

The Directors of FGC were a loyal group of men, some of whom served for many years; Ralph Neville was Chairman until his elevation to the Court of Appeal in 1906 when his place was taken by Aneurin Williams MP (who combined the role with chairmanship of the executive committee of the Land Nationalisation Society) until 1915. Other Directors included industrialists Edward Cadbury, William H Lever and T.H.W. Idris, civil engineer Howard D Pearsall and newspaper proprietor Thomas P Ritzema. Company Secretary Thomas Adams and Manager Ebenezer Howard were also Directors.

The prospectus stated that the Company would *"not only promote a great social improvement, but provide for those who could afford to wait an investment which will prove a sound one"*. *"The root idea…is to deal at once with the two vital questions of overcrowding in our towns and the depopulation of our rural districts…"* The first £80,000 capital was sought from investors in an initial offer of 16,000 shares at £5 and 3000 shares at £1, with a dividend limited to 5 per cent. This was to ensure the Company's primary objective, rather than encouraging speculation in the shares. *"The directors of the company, and the great majority of the shareholders, [were] public-spirited men who had embarked upon the undertaking with the idea of performing a public service…"*, said Charles Purdom, an early recruit to FGC Ltd's administrative staff and its later chronicler. *"The intention was to develop the town in the interests of its future inhabitants, and to secure to those inhabitants…the results of the prosperity of the place."* The early prospectuses did not seek to appeal to the general public because of the unlikelihood of an early return on investment and it was the Directors and their friends who raised half of this amount, which was allocated to part payment of the estate and the initial layout plan. The freehold of the land was mortgaged and by the end of 1904 about £100,000 had been subscribed. However, the pace then slowed considerably and ten years later only £181,026 had been secured. The Pioneer Company had raised money easily because of public goodwill towards the novelty and moral rightness of the garden city scheme but First Garden City's share offer was regarded more sceptically by serious investors. The fact that the dividend was limited to five per cent was not attractive to those simply aiming to make money. As it turned out, a first dividend, of only 1 per cent, was not paid until 1913, it was suspended during the First World War and the 5 per cent maximum was only achieved in 1923. (The arrears of the dividend were paid in full in 1946.) There were further efforts at raising capital through periodic offers to existing shareholders and their friends of debenture and preference shares, notably to finance the construction of the vital utility works.

What First Garden City Ltd needed in order to bring its plan to fruition was publicity, influence over the opinion formers of the day, moral support and, crucially, cash investment. It was this last that was to prove so difficult to achieve and it might be argued that the Company's chronic lack of capital certainly altered the eventual form of the Garden City. (For instance, much of the early housebuilding was done not by the Company but by private individuals and businesses such as J. M. Dent, seeking to provide for their own workers.) The Letchworth estate was revalued in 1907 (for the year ending 1906) which revealed a capital surplus but (Mervyn Miller states) the Directors seemed overly cautious in showing this in the accounts and thereby offered a more gloomy picture of the Company's financial affairs.

"Arms and the Man" cartoon by Louis Weirter, brother -in-law of Thomas Adams. This is one of a series of cartoons by Weirter which were published in The Citizen newspaper, c.1909.

Promoting the Garden City

A variety of promotional methods was used to raise money and to attract businesses to the town, such as personal contacts, newspaper and journal advertisements and brochures issued by FGC entitled *"Letchworth as a manufacturing centre"* and *"Why manufacturers move to Letchworth"*. The Local Government Board disapproved of this type of local promotion as it was regarded as not a proper function of local authorities! Ebenezer Howard continued as a Director but his strength was as a public speaker not as an organizer (although his nominal role was Manager) He summed up the appeal of the garden city concept thus: *"Special advantages should be offered to manufacturers and their employees such as railway sidings, inexpensive land (permitting of one-story factories), cheap power, plenty of light, pure air, houses with good gardens attached, at rent low as compared with those of the crowded city, and in healthy surroundings near to the work and play of the workers... He [the manufacturer] … must…see…a sound business proposition"*. Certainly, a number of the early manufacturers who moved their operations to Letchworth had heard Howard speak at public meetings and been enthused by his rhetoric but their social motivation had to be balanced by a good commercial proposition. In fact, between 1850 and 1945 a large number of foreign companies acquired or established factories in Britain. In the nine years from 1900, 25 foreign companies set up their first British factory, mostly coming from the United States but also from Germany, Sweden and Switzerland. By the beginning of the twentieth century many of the older industries in Britain were in decline and the newer enterprises of engineering, electricity and motor vehicles were seeking new locations and workforces. With improved distribution from the railway network they were less tied to existing manufacturing towns and there emerged the now familiar concept of multi-national and multi-site businesses. Under the 1907 Patent Act a foreign patent taken out in England and Wales had to be worked there to be valid, which encouraged direct investment by foreign companies. Firms saw several advantages to operating in Britain, including a free trade regime up to 1914, and managerial, technological and entrepreneurial opportunities. From 1905 the Company could supply water and gas from its own facilities and electricity from 1907. The decision was taken to prioritise the latter to the industrial areas of the town and some residential homes did not get electricity until the 1940s.

It is illuminating to analyse FGC's records of mortgages, which began to be raised from 1905 using company-built infrastructure such as the water works and electricity power station as security. In that year (additional) mortgage borrowing was £8,000, by 1913 it was £39,891 and by 1920 the total sum owed by the Company (including an overdraft) was £191,497. (This is calculated by the Bank of England inflation calculator at £8,623,420 in 2019.) Relatively small amounts of the overdraft provided by the London Joint City and Midland Bank were repaid each year. FGC had built some of the earliest factory buildings – those occupied by the Lacre and Phoenix car makers and the Meredew furniture manufacturer – so these, as well as certain ground rents and assets such as machinery were used as security for loans.

Early investors

It can be argued that the people most vital to the eventual success of Letchworth were Thomas Adams (Secretary of the Garden City Association and later Company Secretary of First Garden City Ltd), Ralph Neville (Chairman of the Garden City Association) and, later, Walter Gaunt, Estate Manager from 1905–1917. Gaunt was well aware that Letchworth was competing against towns like Luton and Watford in trying to attract new industries so he adopted American-style advertising techniques like billboards. He played down the social policies of Letchworth and emphasised the commercial advantages in the publicity material he sent abroad to the USA, France and Germany, for example, claiming *"[the] best location in England for manufacturers is the new industrial town of Letchworth (Garden City)."*

So, who were the early investors in the garden city and what was their motivation for putting their money (amounts both large and small) into an untried venture? They fall into six broad groups, with an overlapping membership, often linked by political affiliation and Quakerism. Perhaps the most significant and useful investors were the philanthropists. George and Edward Cadbury, father and son of the famous chocolate manufacturing enterprise, were early supporters as were Joseph and Benjamin Rowntree whose Bournville Village Trust provided a loan. Both these families had developed "model" estates for their own workers as fellow investor William H Lever, the wealthy soap manufacturer, also did. A similar group consisted of those who simply wished the project well, such as Edward Talbot, Bishop of Rochester, Thomas Ritzema, newspaper proprietor and protégé of Edward Cadbury, and Aneurin Williams MP, a Middlesborough ironmaster and Chairman of the executive committee of the Land Nationalisation Society. These were men who were able to buy quite substantial numbers of shares with no need of an immediate return.

An important group of shareholders were manufacturers who not only invested money in First Garden City but, in some cases, moved their businesses to Letchworth. Max Herz, who had heard Howard speak in London and become a friend, built a factory for his Swiss embroidery business as did T. H.W. Idris (who was a Director of FGC Ltd and a Liberal MP) for his mineral water plant. Edmund Hunter funded the building of his own weaving works from family money. Franklin Thomasson, a Lancashire cotton spinner, was a major shareholder. Of course, it was a requirement that Directors also hold shares in the Company. George Cadbury and Idris were long-standing members of the Garden City Association, as was Thomas Adams, although he only held four shares!

Influential shareholders were, in many cases, friends of Ebenezer Howard. H G Wells had met him at a Zetetical [debating] Society meeting in 1879 and was wealthy enough to buy a large block of shares. Another investor friend was George Bernard Shaw. Henry Rider Haggard is best known as a prolific and popular author but he was also a Norfolk landowner, gentleman farmer and agricultural experimenter. Although politically far apart from his friend Ebenezer Howard, he was a shareholder in, and supporter of, Letchworth who had published, in 1902, a two-volume survey of the state of agriculture in England with suggestions for reforms. He attended a number of the Arbor [tree planting] Days held in the town. Rider Haggard may have alerted the Company to the loans available under the various Land Improvement Acts from the General Land and Drainage Improvement Company. Surprisingly, Eliza Howard, Ebenezer's first wife, held 753 shares, a comparatively large holding. A final group were the co-operative societies which bought varying numbers of shares in a project which, presumably, they wished to support with no guarantee of a worthwhile return.

A distinguishing feature of Howard's proposal for a garden city was the principle of the common ownership of land and that any rise in the value of the town's estate – the so-called *"unearned increment"* – would be retained for the benefit of the community. One of Thomas Adams' fundraising tactics was to solicit investment from people such as George Lansbury, later to be leader of the Labour Party, and the American soap magnate Joseph Fels who were known to be supporters of a land value tax. An independent valuation undertaken for the Company in September 1907 calculated that the estate's expenses (the purchase of the land and investment in its infrastructure) amounted to £247,806 13s 11d whilst the town as it then existed was valued at £379,500. The Directors found this reassuring. However, from a purely business point of view this novel idea was a flaw (notably pointed out by George Bernard Shaw to Ralph Neville) that would impede attracting investment from capitalists. And so it proved, as capital was painfully slow to accrue. By the end of the Company's first year only £100,000 had been raised from shareholders and by the autumn of 1906, when Thomas Adams left, the capital was £148,000, less than the purchase price of £155,000. By then over £200,000 had been expended on the town's infrastructure, financed by loans and mortgages. Walter Gaunt, the new Estate Manager, had been recruited because of his success at the industrial estate of Trafford Park, Manchester, (begun in 1898) and adopted a severely commercial approach with higher ground rents, cheaper housing and rapid industrialisation. For this he received criticism from the idealists.

In conclusion, it is clear that the path from Ebenezer Howard's initial ideas, expressed in his 1898 book *To-Morrow: A Peaceful Path to Real Reform*, to the marking out of the plots of land for the First Garden City was by no means smooth. The financial model chosen by the first Directors relied heavily on private investment; this was not an era of government subsidy. It is a tribute to those early philanthropists and supporters who kept faith with the garden city ideal that it became the success it is and, seemingly, a model for future developments in Britain and across the world.

Front cover of a programme promoting the annual Shareholders and Members visit to Letchworth, July 1907.

STARTING DEVELOPMENT AT LETCHWORTH

The purchase of the larger pieces of land forming the Letchworth estate had been completed by 25 September 1903 and by May 1904 so too the remaining smaller areas. This meant that by late spring 1904 the Company owned the majority of the estate within the necessary ring fence to commence development. The only exception at that time was reported as a fourteen-acre field held by the Arlesey Lime Company.

The initial issue of the Company's shares (16,000 £5 ordinary shares) was intended to raise £80,000, which was to be used for part payment of the land acquisition (along with residual capital from the Pioneer Company) and the remainder of the purchase cost of £155,587 was to remain on mortgage. This was meant to be a short-term measure as the Directors' Report of May 1904 set out an intention to repay this with the release of the remaining shares within six months, as well as providing funds for development. This ambitious intent simply did not materialise and in fact much of the initial purchase money remained on mortgage beyond 1920, along with additional borrowing to support capital investment as development progressed.

The relentless demand for capital to support development and associated growth far outweighed what could realistically be expected of even their wealthiest shareholders. Instead the Company relied increasingly on additional borrowing provided through new mortgages and loans secured on estate assets, alongside this.

By 30 September 1904 the Company owed £83,391 on mortgage (equivalent to £10,277,098 in 2019) and by the same date in 1920 loans and mortgages had increased to £181,372 (£8,167,475 in 2019). Over those sixteen years First Garden City managed to repay £76,000, despite additional borrowing of £149,185. From 1915 the Company used overdraft facilities provided by its bankers – London Joint City & Midland Bank Ltd. – which were secured against the gas, water and electricity utilities. Nevertheless, at the end of 1916 the amount owed on the overdraft alone was £23,835 (£2,088,862 in 2019), although this was cleared by the end of 1918. The Company ended the decade, in 1920, with overdraft borrowing of £10,124 (£455,900 in 2019).

The need for borrowing was exacerbated by a much slower than hoped for take up of share issues. There was limited repayment of borrowing during the early years and the amounts repaid varied year on year, although the largest repayments were made in 1912, 1916 and 1917. Given the scale of such an ambitious building project this does not seem surprising now and the costs pale into insignificance against today's large construction projects!

Accounts of Letchworth tell of a struggle for capital and that this impeded development but one account by Harold Craske, Secretary of FGC Ltd, written in 1926, states that Directors successfully found capital when it was needed (even if it was just in time). This is borne out by the financial records of the Company and also comments made by Henry Blackwell Harris (as Chairman) in 1920. Craske reported that the lack of capital may actually have been beneficial and prevented costly mistakes. Directors, he said, also felt that a tightness of capital kept development schemes steady. On many occasions during the first decade of Letchworth's development Directors reported that more could have been achieved if more capital had been available. However, maybe just as Craske commented in 1926, the steady rate of capital was just what was needed.

The evidence points to a well-managed development process, balancing investment and spending priorities with available resources. Whether this was achieved within the original timescales is almost irrelevant given what was achieved by the Directors of First Garden City

Ltd (in such as relatively short time frame). This is examined further below and is what should be celebrated as the great achievement at Letchworth. If properly understood and appreciated it likely would be the envy of many development companies today.

Well planned and executed

The most astonishing thing about Letchworth's development was the pace at which this new industrial town began to emerge. Remember, the estate was largely agricultural in nature yet within eighteen months of purchase (spring 1905) the key infrastructure was in place, including houses, some factories and other facilities. This was all carefully planned and overseen by the Directors of First Garden City Ltd, supported by their architects and engineers. Of particular note is the care taken at the start of the project to ensure the right sequence of development work. From the outside it may have looked as if little was happening but behind the scenes there was lots of initial activity to get things right. Indeed, in the *Guide to Garden City* published by the Garden City Press in spring 1905 this was covered in the first section, explaining the vast amount of work behind the scenes.

Guide to Garden City – promotional guide book published by the Garden City Press Ltd, early 1905.

It took six months (from September 1903) to secure the purchase of the entirety of the estate. This involved careful negotiations, including consideration of the relationship with existing tenants. As well as successfully getting the necessary ring fence of land the Directors also negotiated favourable new arrangements with existing tenants. These enabled tenants to remain on the land until such time as the Company required it for development, which obviously provided a source of rental income while the estate was planned and early developments progressed. More importantly, they included a clause which enabled the Company to take possession for development at any time and with reduced compensation payments.

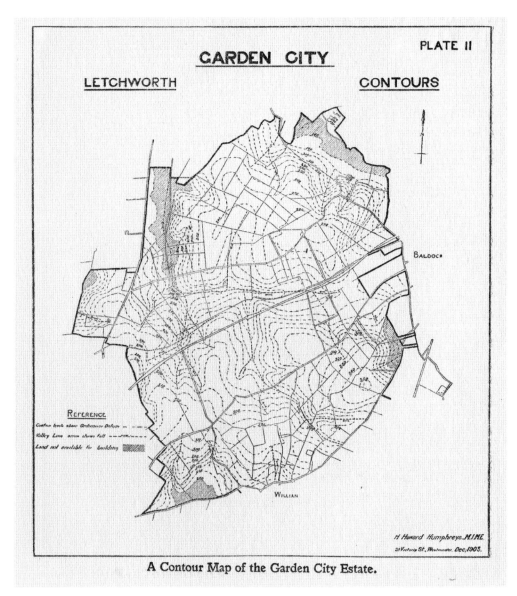

A Contour Map of the Garden City Estate.

October 1903 – March 1904: The first six months – sorting the estate plan

Responding to company shareholders in April 1904 as to why Directors had not been trying to secure new tenants or manufacturers in the first six months, Company Chairman Ralph Neville explained that it was crucial first to deal with existing tenants and also develop the plan for the city before any land could be let.

Preparing the plan for the new town took six months and was started in October 1903. Poor weather conditions that winter caused some delays to the process. But even before architects could start work on their plan the whole of the estate had to be contour surveyed and this work took almost three months (October–December 1903). It was led by Howard Humphreys, a consulting engineer based in Victoria Street, London, assisted by Alfred Bullmore (later to become the Company's long serving resident engineer). The selected estate plan, prepared by Letchworth's famous architects Barry Parker and Raymond Unwin, was put before Company shareholders at the 20 April 1904 meeting.

Even on this early plan you can see marked the existing and first new roads to be developed.

THE FIRST GARDEN CITY—PLAN OF ESTATE AND PROPOSED TOWN.

(NOTE.—The Plan of the Town, which has been designed by Messrs. Barry Parker and Raymond Unwin, Architects, Baldock, is, of course, subject to modification and further development.)

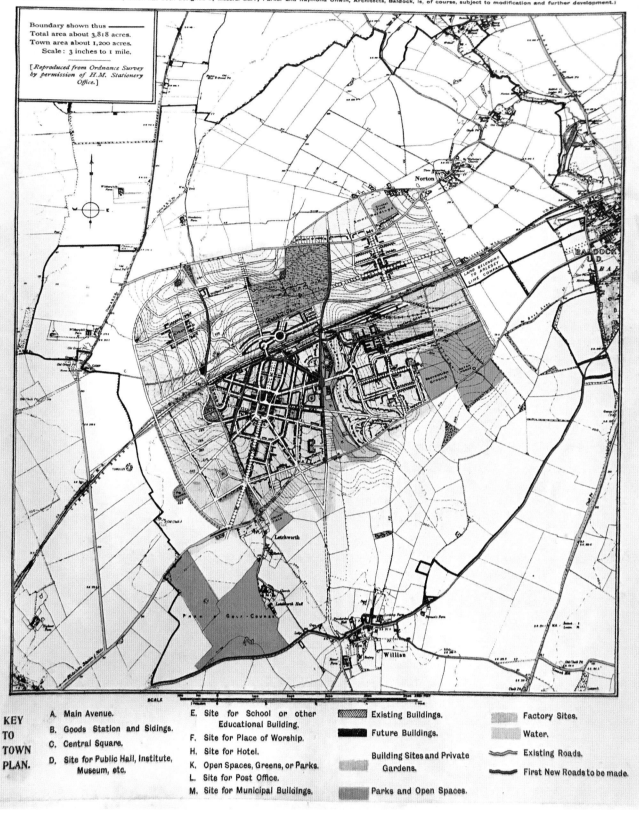

Boundary shown thus ————
Total area about 3,818 acres.
Town area about 1,200 acres.
Scale: 3 inches to 1 mile.

[Reproduced from Ordnance Survey by permission of H.M. Stationery Office.]

KEY
TO
TOWN
PLAN.

A. Main Avenue.
B. Goods Station and Sidings.
C. Central Square.
D. Site for Public Hall, Institute, Museum, etc.
E. Site for School or other Educational Building.
F. Site for Place of Worship.
H. Site for Hotel.
K. Open Spaces, Greens, or Parks.
L. Site for Post Office.
M. Site for Municipal Buildings.

Existing Buildings.
Future Buildings.
Building Sites and Private Gardens.
Parks and Open Spaces.
Factory Sites.
Water.
Existing Roads.
First New Roads to be made.

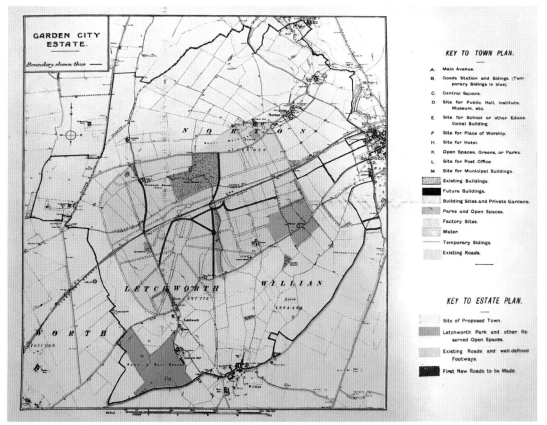

Set of three plans produced by Parker and Unwin and published by First Garden City Ltd as the approved plans for the estate in April 1904 – showing varying levels of detail.

The Directors were clear from the outset that even though this early plan had been adopted it would be subject to modifications as development progressed. The Garden City Collection has a number of town plans published over time by First Garden City Ltd.. These plans provide a useful timeline as to the sequence of development and how the town took shape.

In their 1904 report to shareholders the Directors also acknowledged the engineers' contributions, stating that the plan wasn't just the work of the architects, as consideration had to be given to a number of engineering matters and other questions. These included:

- Sites for railway, railway goods siding [sic] and factories – these had to be assessed in relation to each other and to the main thoroughfares for the town.

- The need to preserve an area of open space around the waterworks – the Directors had also sunk a well to satisfy themselves as to whereabouts on the estate they would be able to obtain an ample supply of water.

- The site of the town had to be thought about in relation to the question of drainage as well as preserving features of the estate.

This underlines the contribution of others to the planning of Letchworth. Each of these issues was carefully considered and resolved during this planning process. The expertise of each of the engineers ensured that the location, design and development of the key infrastructure was correct, to be able to support the town and its industry.

- Howard Humphreys – led the work to develop the contour plan for the whole estate, assisted by Alfred Bullmore.

- George Richardson Strachan – FGC Ltd's consulting engineer for water, sewerage and roads. Strachan was also involved during the site selection phase. Unfortunately, he died, aged 51, in September 1907 and Alfred Bullmore (who assisted Strachan) took over as the Company's consulting engineer.

- Alfred Bullmore – had a long and successful career with FGC Ltd; a press article from the 1930s celebrates 25 years long service when he was still continuing in his role. Bullmore was also Fire Chief on two separate occasions.

- Edward Parry and Frederick William Bidder – also based in Victoria Street, London (and Nottingham) were FGC Ltd's consulting engineers for railway construction.

- Sir Corbett Woodhall, one of the most respected gas engineers of his time, who prepared a preliminary report for FGC Ltd in 1903 and Charles Hunt, Consulting Gas Engineer, responsible for planning and overseeing development of the gas works in 1904–1905.

- Messrs O'Gorman and Cuzens Hardy – Consulting Engineers, based in Westminster, were responsible for planning and overseeing development of the Central Power Station in 1907.

June 1904 – December 1904: Orderly works and controlled letting of sites

The Directors set out a clear order of work needed before any significant site letting to manufacturers. These were:

- To lay two to three miles of road, part permanent, part temporary – with a view to connecting the two main roads which intersect the northern and southern parts of the estate parallel to the railway. These roads were marked red on the early development plan prepared by Parker and Unwin. The road works were detailed in the Directors' report which stated the planned expenditure of £2,000–3,000 would add value to the estate as well improving connectivity and accessibility of key points on the estate at that time.

- To carry out a water scheme – construction of pumping station, water works and reservoir. The first bore hole was sunk in the early part of winter 1903 when it was planned to pump water one mile to a reservoir situated on Weston Hills (construction of which started in June 1904 and was completed by late summer). It was agreed about the same time also to supply water to Baldock Urban District Council.

- To provide a supply of gas to the first residents and manufacturers and at a later date an electricity supply.

- Initial main drainage scheme – from Letchworth via Baldock Road and the new North Road to the temporary sewage farm (situated on a bed of gravel and chalk considerably north of the railway). This would provide for a population of between three and four thousand at a capital cost of around £3,000. This temporary sewage farm served the town for just under 20 years!

Work underway to construct the main drainage scheme, 1904.

The Company had to invest £20,000 in these capital works before the town would be in a position for any large influx of manufacturers and population. Directors expected to be able to complete the water and sewerage works within six months and be ready for the first manufacturers by the end of 1904. The water engineer, G R Strachan, started work in December 1903 as soon as the contour plan was completed.

Looking at construction projects today, this seems wildly ambitious but this was achieved and by mid-December 1904 the greater part of these early construction works were nearing completion. However, proactive letting of sites didn't take place until spring 1905 and even this was much quicker than initially anticipated. One thing that is apparent is the care Directors took to ensure they did not over promise and under deliver as this would have had a significant negative impact on the reputation of the scheme at such an early stage.

The first Estate Office was opened in April 1904 and even though there was a healthy demand for sites from the start (some 200–300 applications had been received) lettings were initially restricted to shareholders of the Company. Directors wanted to progress on well-established lines avoiding unnecessary and speculative expenditure, noting a need to *"avoid too much risk early on by large expenditure on public works, large numbers of dwellings or factories"*.

Interestingly, the Directors wanted to allow the residential area of the town outside of workers' housing to take root. The reason for this was given as wanting to secure as natural as possible a method of growth and enable the Company to achieve increased revenue without any large capital expenditure or sacrificing of its principles. They also categorically stated it did not represent a departure from the proposal to create an industrial rather than residential town.

First Estate Office opened by First Garden City Ltd., April 1904.

Key milestones

- A temporary railway station was built and operating, but with a restricted service; it was completed in less than one month in September 1903, in time for the Estate Opening in early October 1903. Full passenger services did not begin operating until spring 1905, with the first ticket recorded as being issued on 15 April 1905. The buildings of the temporary station were constructed by Messrs Wilmott of Hitchin.

- New siding, adjacent to the factory area was built by the Great Northern Railway Company, also a supporter and shareholder in the Letchworth venture. The siding was designed to serve around 120 acres of factories and works sites. It was used to transport much needed building materials to the estate.

- The underground Weston Hills Reservoir was completed by October 1904.

- Road laying was undertaken by the Company using labour provided by the unemployed men sent to Letchworth from London. It is reported that 1,000 tonnes of brick rubble arrived at Letchworth in early July 1904 for road making.

- Factory sites selected:
  - Garden City Press Ltd
  - Heatly Gresham Engineering Company, London and Royston
  - A. Wilmer Collier Esq, stationery manufacturer, London
  - Messrs Idris & Co, mineral water manufacturer
  - Messrs Ewart & Co, geyser manufacturers London
  - Vickers & Field, asphalt manufacturers, London.

First Garden City Ltd railway sidings used for transportation of materials and goods.

Road laying – said to be an image of the digging out of Birds Hill, Letchworth, c.1903.

Spring 1905 – getting ready for the industries

By the spring of 1905 the key infrastructure was almost complete, with the main access routes, drainage and sewerage scheme, water supply, railway station and factory siding finished. Construction of the town's gas works was also well under way and it was operating by late summer 1905. Provision of gas for industry and homes had been prioritised over electricity, which came in 1907. All this development had been achieved in a little over a year since the Board of Directors approved Parker and Unwin's Town Plan!

At this point it is important to say more about the contribution of hundreds of unemployed men sent from London to help out with building the early infrastructure (drainage, mains laying, road-building, etc.) at Letchworth. According to an account in the *Guide to Garden City*, published around spring 1905, up to 400 unemployed men were employed by FGC Ltd at Letchworth to help with the early period of development. The men were well provided for, with accommodation and pay at the going rate for construction work offered by the Company.

These unemployed men were part of early labour schemes set up to tackle localised unemployment. In the case of Letchworth, they were sent by the Central Committee for the Unemployed, based in London, and by the West Ham Committee.

London workmen sent by the London Unemployed Committee to help with the construction of Letchworth, c.1905, photographed outside "the Sheds", Nevells Road.

Over 250 men were housed in purpose-built accommodation at the west end of what is now Nevells Road. The buildings were known locally as "the Sheds" and were constructed partly from wood and partly from "Calmon Asbestos" in a short space of time by the garden city's own pioneer builders, Messrs Picton and Hope. The Sheds included accommodation and mess room facilities. The latter used to hold regular Sunday evening lectures for the men, which were planned by a committee of garden city residents. Committee members included Mr. and Mrs. Raymond Unwin and Mr. Howard Pearsall (Company Director). There were concerts and social gatherings on weekday evenings, providing entertainment for the men and residents of the neighbouring towns of Hitchin and Baldock.

The remaining 100 men lived in a disused malthouse in Baldock which had been rented for three months and kitted out with beds, bedding and kitchen equipment provided by the Salvation Army at a reduced cost. According to reports of the time, the men referred to the accommodation at Baldock as "Hotel Cecil", likely to be a witty comparison to the luxury surroundings of the Hotel Cecil in central London at that time.

Of the men at Baldock 80 came from West Ham and 20 came from Walthamstow and formed a smaller labour colony set up by the West Ham Board of Guardians and Borough Council. Geoffrey Christie-Miller (of the Christy Hat Company and also an FGC Ltd shareholder), Gerrard Collier and Edward Howarth collectively raised £800 for this scheme and a report prepared by them on the outcome of the men's time at Letchworth is held in the British Library. The men worked eight-hour days for which they received board and lodging as well as 6d a week for tobacco and grants for wives and children back at home. The report states that as a result of good food and clean air the physical condition of the men improved. Despite the best efforts of Ebenezer Howard and others, many of the men were not persuaded to settle in Letchworth or find permanent work locally; just over one per cent did! The men worked at digging two artificial lakes (probably at Howard Park) as well as helping with road building; both tasks were difficult due to the wet conditions at the time.

The men were in Letchworth during February, March and April 1905, after which the Sheds were converted in May 1905 into exhibition buildings for the 1905 Cheap Cottages Exhibition which opened on 25 July 1905. Land adjoining the mess room became a pleasure garden for visitors to the exhibition, with a tea room provided. After the Exhibition, the Sheds provided temporary accommodation for a number of the industries while they got established or had

premises built. Dent, Spirella, Marmet, Slater & Co and AC Furmston (the latter two were engineering companies) all made use of these facilities as necessary. These temporary buildings actually lasted until the mid-1930s when they were finally demolished.

Although there was a great demand for labour due to development of the town, there was also a chronic lack of suitable accommodation available in the new garden city. With hindsight it is easy to be critical of the early decision of Directors to focus on encouraging residential development (outside of accommodation for workers). Perhaps this explains why one of the colony founders and funders paid for the building of six cottages at Letchworth. Six of the 26 cottages built on Birds Hill (then known as Station Road East) for workers of Heatly Gresham were funded by Geoffrey Christie-Miller. He also paid for or sponsored other cottages (including prize winning cottages in the 1907 Urban Cottages Exhibition) throughout the garden city. Christie-Miller also established St Helen's Convalescent home (now Noel House on Norton Way North), having seen the needs of poor children in West Ham, London. Resolving the lack of housing provision for labourers and workers was a continuing challenge for the Company.

Interior of the Sheds – sleeping quarters for the workmen.

Interior of the Sheds – dining quarters for the workmen.

The earliest pioneer industries

The first industry at work on the estate was Vickers and Field, manufacturers of asphalt products, operating from temporary sheds from December 1904. Given the significant development underway, their materials and products would have been in demand at the time. They later became Permalite Ltd with more permanent works being built. Vickers and Field won a prize for their "Wirebitu" (damp proof membrane) product in the 1905 Cheap Cottages Exhibition.

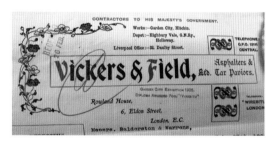

Company letterhead - Vickers & Field, dated July 1905. Note the Garden City, Hitchin, address given at the top.

The Garden City Press Ltd printers were actually established a year before Vickers and Field in December 1903 but operated out of temporary works in Bancroft, Hitchin (on premises in the yard of Messrs Geo. W. Russell & Son). After just seven months, GC Press had a workforce of 22 and were very proud to be part of the garden city experiment, promoting their status as the first business established in connection with the new garden city. They were delayed in their move from Hitchin until November 1905, because of a devastating fire which burnt their initial wooden printworks to the ground on 24 August 1905. This happened just weeks before they were due to relocate and on the day that manager Bert Williams and his colleague were at a national co-partnership event. Such was their resolve that they commenced rebuilding immediately, constructing a brick printworks on the same foundations. This was completed within two months, with support from sympathetic co-partners.

By the summer of 1905 the works for Heatly Gresham Engineers was also built and they were at work, employing 80 men and by the end of the following year more than doubling the size of their works and workforce to over 200 men!

The employment provided by these early firms, along with people who were already established at Letchworth, meant that the population had pretty much tripled in almost two years since the opening of the estate. This is quite remarkable, especially as FGC Ltd only started systematically advertising sites to let from early 1905. Public appeals for more capital were also avoided until development on the estate was more advanced. Again, this was entirely sensible as no doubt the Company would be judged on what people could see.

Other building- and construction-related businesses also had premises in the industrial area, including Messrs Eastwood, brick manufacturers, who had a brick-storing facility and Ellis and Everard who were timber merchants. The location would have been ideal for these businesses with delivery of building materials made easy from the adjacent railway sidings.

Workers outside Vickers & Field Asphalt works, Letchworth.

Aftermath of the fire in August 1905 which devastated the first wooden Garden City Press works building at Letchworth, and delayed their move from Hitchin.

Advertisement for the Garden City Press, shows the rebuilt works this time of a brick construction!

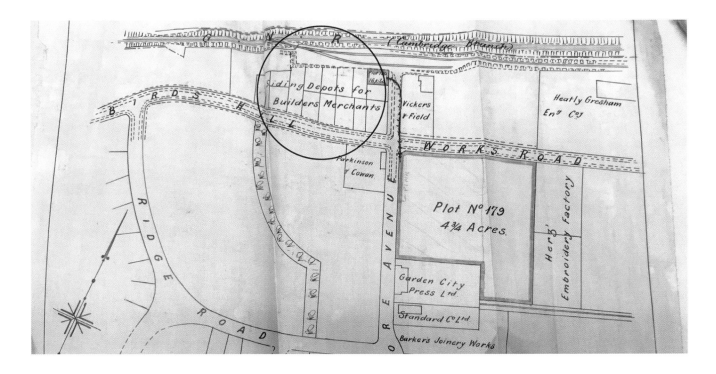

Extract from W. H. Smith & Son plot file (c.1906) which shows plots set aside for builders merchants adjacent railway siding (ringed).

By October 1906 the number of factories at work or in the course of erection had increased significantly:

Heatly Gresham Engineering Co Ltd – operating and extended
Garden City Press Ltd. – operating
Vickers & Field – operating
Idris & Co Ltd – under construction
G Ewart & Sons – under construction
The Standard Co Ltd – operating
Garden City Embroidery – under construction
Messrs Brooks & Co Instrument makers – unclear whether operating or under construction
Wheeler, Odell & Co Printers – operating (from temporary premises in Green Lane)
W. H. Smith & Son bookbinders – under construction
J. M. Dent & Co – under construction
Arden Press – under construction

Factory leases

The Company's policy initially was to offer tenants the option of Ordinary Lease or Perpetual Lease terms and all lessees (whether industrial or residential) were given three months at peppercorn rent and a timescale within which building work was to be completed (including when temporary buildings had to be replaced with more permanent factories or works). The variation in lease terms is evidenced in the archive material available on plot files held by the Garden City Collection.

- Idris & Co – 99 Years

- Garden City Press – 999 Years

- J. M. Dent – 99 years

- W. H. Smith & Son – 99 years

- Vickers & Co – 60 years with option to renew for another 60 years.

Some of the early leases were also granted for initial terms, e.g., the Iceni Pottery lease was for seven years from June 1908 with option to renew for a further 92 years.

By 1913 (as reported by C B Purdom in *The Garden City*), leases were granted on one of the following terms:

- 99 years at a fixed rent
- 999 years at a rent revisable every 99 years
- 999 years at a rent revisable every 10 years
- and (for factories only) 999 years at a fixed rent.

The leases contained a series of covenants (requirements) which had to be complied with and these included:

- to build within a reasonable timeframe, to the approval of Architect or Surveyor of FGC Ltd
- value of buildings to be erected was specified
- contribution to road maintenance costs
- contribution to costs of making and maintaining party walls, fences, hedges, gutters, sewers and drains which belonged to or were used in connection with the industrial premises
- to keep the premises, including grounds/gardens well maintained
- insurance for all buildings against loss or damage by fire
- controls around advertisements – for example sky-line, green field and some illuminated adverts were not permitted
- use of FGC Ltd utilities – gas, power, water.

Factory Lease Agreement.

Form used by First Garden City Ltd to capture details regarding factory leases.

There were also standard requirements around right of access (for FGC Ltd) and right to repair etc.

The Company claimed that leases enabled manufacturers to pay annual ground rents and thereby invest their capital in the business itself rather than the land. FGC Ltd did build a number of factories which manufacturers could purchase on mortgage – Lacre, Phoenix and Meredew all took advantage of this option. In 1920, reflecting back on this, the Company said that the majority of manufacturers were unwilling to build themselves and preferred to rent premises, due to a shortage of working capital and not wanting to tie it up in bricks and mortar. Where this was a short-term issue the Company felt that by granting mortgages to suitable manufacturers this could be overcome. This approach probably helped attract firms who would otherwise not have been able to move.

PROGRESS ON THE ESTATE: ROAD-MAKING AND INFRASTRUCTURE

Capital expenditure

The following table from the FGC accounts illustrates the amount of capital invested by the Company in the making up, laying out and surfacing of new roads as development progressed. Up to 30th September 1915, FGC Ltd spent £53,387 on highways in Letchworth (around £5.5m today), more than half of which they spent during the first five years.

They also had to maintain existing roads so there was additional revenue expenditure on maintenance work.

Year	Amount	New roads listed
1904	£3,157	North Road (Norton Way) Station Road Acacia Avenue Pixmore Road Spring Road Conference Road Dunhams Lane (existed) Green Lane Icknield Way Baldock Road
1905	£9,062	Ploughmans Road Ridge Road Exhibition Roads [sic] Barrington Road Meadow Way Glebe Road Common View Road Letchworth Glade Letchworth Railways siding Temporary road to cattle creep
1906	£5,377	Leys Avenue Sollershott West Pixmore Way Middle Street (Lytton Avenue) Field Lane Garth Avenue (funded by Arthur Bates) Baldock Road – paths, avenue trees and road margins
1907	£6,799	Main Avenue (Broadway) Hillside The Leys (Gernon Road) North Fork Avenue South Fork (Common View) Dents Road (at Dunhams Lane)

		Bridge over railway Commerce Avenue Rushby Mead Hillshott Pixmore Hill (Broughton Hill) Ridge Avenue
1908	£3,932	New Icknield Way Sollershott East Pixmore Hill Broadway
1909	£3,814	-
1910	£2,229	Station Place & Way Town Square Eastcheap Broadwater Avenue Lytton Avenue South View The Meads Barrington Road Willian Way
1911	£6,721	Shott Lane Allington Lane Works Road Bruce Wallace Road
1912	£3,845	Boscombe Place Saw Mills Road The Wynd Cashio Lane
1913	£3,046	Souberie Avenue Bridge Road School Walk Glebe Road to Common View Road
1914	No Company Accounts available	
1915	£1,608	Cromwell Green Valley Way The Dale Cross Street The Quadrant The Dale East Burnell Walk Campers Square Paddock Close Burnell Rise

1916	£1,201	Campers Road Campers Walk
1917	£856	West View Woodworkers Road Connecting road – Glebe Road to Icknield Way Co-operative Road Commerce Avenue
1918	negligible	-
1919	£270	Covered half the cost of the material used in altering and laying double line sidings to the Kryn & Lahy Works
1920	£4,063	Storm water sewer works (New Icknield Way) and storm drains (Common View) Commerce Lane construction

The first roads laid and surfaced included the main thoroughfares for the town to ensure connectivity and access around key areas of the estate. Dunhams Lane was one of the few roads which already existed on the estate when it was newly purchased. Laying out of roads and other necessary infrastructure was undertaken only when it made sense in line with progress of development across the estate.

Road surfaces were not of a quality we know today, and even when completed most were no more than tracks with gravel surfaces. Digging and laying out of roads would have been hard work without modern mechanical tools. The unemployed workmen who came from London carried out much of this work in the first year or so.

The Company also made roads to service factories and other works, including Woodworkers Road, Co-operatives Road, Pearsall Warne Road and Saw Mills Road, and part-invested in extensions to factory sidings. This suggests a fairly relaxed approach to naming some of the less formal accesses and roads.

View from Birds Hill looking towards Station Road. To the right are some of the cottages for workers at Heatly Gresham Engineering – designed by the architect Victor Dunkerley and built by local builders Picton and Hope, spring 1905.

*The two images show
work underway laying
out roads on the estate,
c.1904/05.*

One interesting anecdote from the 1906 accounts refers to a Mr. Bates, who is recorded as having made and paid for the construction of Garth Avenue. The 1911 Census records an Arthur Bates and his family living on Garth Road, so surely this is him? No further information or explanation is given but maybe he got tired of waiting for a decent access road to his house.

Road names

Looking around Letchworth today there are many roads with links to Letchworth's foundation as a garden city – including the early industries, architects and builders. There is Lacre Way, Meredews, Arden Press Way, Ascot Drive, Openshaw Way and Dunkerley Court to name a few. However, others are inspired by much earlier historical references. These include Barrington Road – supposedly named after Edward Barrington who purchased the Letchworth estate from the Knights Hospitaller in the reign of Henry IV – and Gernon Road – named after Robert Gernon, a French Norman duke and relation of William the Conquerer.

Over time some early road names also changed, such as:

North Road – Norton Way North and South
Exhibition Road – Nevells Road
Middle Street – Lytton Avenue
Main Avenue – Broadway
The Leys – Gernon Road
Acacia Avenue – Broadwater Avenue

Others are a little more puzzling, like Bruce Wallace Road which could simply be an early name for what became the Quadrant, as the Reverend J Bruce Wallace was an early resident of the new garden city and lived in one of the cottages in the Quadrant.

Laying of sewers, water and gas mains

*Mains piping materials
visible at the Company's
railway sidings in the
industrial area.*

Completed as part of the essential infrastructure works and alongside the making of roads was the laying of many miles of pipework for sewers, water and gas mains. Early images in the Garden City Collection show development underway, including cottage building, and often you can see evidence of this work, with piles of pipes stacked along the road.

The sidings were used to receive and store materials which would then be transported around the estate as needed. This work, although essential, would have been expensive in terms of labour and materials so capital costs were minimised by laying sewers and mains as needed as development advanced across the estate.

Progress is recorded in the archives and this incremental approach is evident in the figures:

Cumulative total laid at end of each year

Year	Sewers	Gas	Water	New roads
1904			5 miles	$1\frac{1}{2}$ miles
1905	4 miles	Gas works open and mains laid along principal routes	12 miles	5 miles
1906	8 miles	8 miles *(gas being supplied to all new homes on estate)*	15 miles *(400 houses connected to water supply)*	$4\frac{1}{2}$ miles
1907	10 miles	10 miles	$15\frac{3}{4}$ miles	$7\frac{3}{4}$ miles
1908	11 miles	12 miles	17 miles	8 miles
1909			$17\frac{1}{2}$ miles	
1910			$18\frac{1}{2}$ miles	
1911	$13\frac{1}{4}$ miles	14 miles	20 miles	$9\frac{1}{2}$ miles
1912			21 miles	
1913		17 miles	21 miles	14 miles

NB: This table is derived from figures published by First Garden City Ltd and other written accounts of progress at Letchworth. Not all accounts covered all the infrastructure aspects in the table, so it is left blank where no information was available.

POPULATION GROWTH AND DEMAND FOR HOUSING

Directors' Reports provide useful information on progress made. During the first year and a quarter (up to January 1905) the population grew by very little, just 100 extra residents. Given the limited residential lettings to that point and that the industries were still to come, this is not surprising. The rate of population growth reflects the influx of industries.

The decision by Company Directors to prioritise letting of residential sites over factory sites is made clear by the number of sites shown as under construction or completed on the early town plans. Figures are also provided in Company reports and press reports of the time. By summer 1905, 300 or so cottage sites had already been let, including those forming part of the 1905 Cheap Cottages Exhibition (131 cottages). Compare this to the position on factory sites where only a handful had been let by the same time. This was not seen as a failure but was, in fact, carefully planned to ensure the infrastructure was ready to support industry.

Calendar years population increase:

- 1905 – up by 1,000
- 1906 – up by 1,500
- 1907 – up by 2,500

By the end of 1907, the numbers of factory workers resident in Letchworth was reported as 900, up from 240 in the previous year. The annual report of Garden City Tenants Ltd (to 31 January 1907) recorded healthy demand for its cottages and that 70 on Birds Hill were let and that 30 more were under construction on Pixmore Hill. For those cottages the society reported that W. H. Smith were to guarantee the rents for ten years and that they would require more cottages in the future.

Due to the lack of suitable accommodation for workers and labourers, many had no option but to commute. The Directors' Report of progress in 1908 refers to *"men at work in Letchworth having to keep their wives and children in London due to the lack of accommodation at Letchworth."* A report in the *Beds Advertiser* of 8 December 1905 on a social gathering held in the Sheds for the workmen employed on the estate, referred to the problem. At that time there were over 500 men at work on the estate, building, making roads, laying sewers, water and gas mains, as well as at work in the first factories, Heatly Gresham and Garden City Press. It was reported that some of those men had a daily fourteen mile round trip, on foot, to work, due to the lack of suitable accommodation in Letchworth. The Dean of St Albans, present at that event, said *"the success of the garden city is dependent on provision of accommodation for the working classes as well as for other classes"*. In April 1906 the Garden City Association wrote of *"the great need for labourers' cottages."*

Growth in Letchworth Population 1903–1920

1903	450
1906	1,500
1907	4,000
1911	5,324
1912	6,000
1914	9,000 (increase due to arrival of Belgian refugees)
1916	Peaked at 13,000
1919	10,000 (following departure of Belgian refugees)
1920	10,500

NB: These figures are mostly estimates made by First Garden City Ltd at the time, with the exception of 1903 and 1911 (based on 1911 Census data). FGC Ltd commented that the 1911 figure recorded by the Census was likely to have been an underestimate as the count happened on Sunday 2 April and many residents would have been out of town.

Of the 300 or so cottage sites let during 1905 very few were suitable for labourers or factory workers. Instead, the demand for residential plots from private investors, those with private means or professionals, really started house building on the estate. Less immediate was the building and provision of sufficient accommodation for labourers and factory workers. This can be directly attributed to a decision by Company Directors to focus on letting of residential sites ahead of those for workers' housing.

By 1906, concentrations of houses and cottages began to be established along the main roads laid out by the Company. This developing pattern can be seen throughout the early town plans of 1905, 1906 and 1908. The Cheap Cottages Exhibition held between July and September 1905 provided a nucleus of residential dwellings, albeit much more suitable for artisans, managers and people of private means than labourers and factory workers. Other cottages and larger villa sites let at that time, which were dotted around the initial access routes, were unaffordable by lower-skilled workers. Residential surveys and Census records show that some better-paid workers did live in cottages not necessarily purposely designed for them.

The Company built a handful of cottages to house its own labourers on the estate in 1904 but outside of this provision was initially left to the market. A few manufacturers built small numbers of houses for their workers (Heatly Gresham and Dent) but the shortage was laid bare with the demand from labourers working on the estate. The situation became much worse as factories were established, becoming most acute in 1906 and 1907, with quite substantial and sudden growth and from then on not really improving much despite the best efforts of Cottage Societies.

Ironically, this lack of accommodation hampered efforts to attract manufacturers and led to overcrowding in those cottages that were available. The 1911 Census shows this, as one of the key aims for a garden city was to deal with the ills of overcrowding in towns. A quotation from an article in the GCA's journal published in August 1915 asserts: *"It is stated that in connection with some of the new factories established at Letchworth, some forty or fifty fresh workers arrive at Letchworth daily."* There is a direct correlation between development on the estate and the growth in industry and the acute shortage of suitable housing for workers faced at Letchworth. Regular progress reports, press cuttings and other publicity sources show just how rapidly the population grew.

The larger the town became the more infrastructure and development took place, which needed labourers. Couple this with the increasing arrival of the industries and it is easy to see how quickly the seriousness of the situation escalated.

Housing societies step up

In 1905 the Garden City Press formed a sister enterprise – Garden City Tenants Ltd – a co-partnership housing society specifically to build cottages for workers in the garden city. They were the first housing society established in Letchworth and followed in the footsteps of other societies encouraged and supported by the co-partnership housing societies movement.

First Garden City Ltd also set up Letchworth Cottages and Buildings Ltd in 1906, working alongside the housing societies and employers to try to solve the shortage and increase provision

Work underway on construction of cottages on Ridge Road, part of the Pixmore Estate built by Garden City Tenants Ltd.

of cottages suitable for labourers and factory workers. They did not build directly, instead working with contractors.

The Company recognised the significant role played by Garden City Tenants Ltd in the provision of housing for workers in the early years. By 1915 the society had built 320 cottages at Letchworth; within their first two years they completed 130 cottages on their developments at Eastholm Green (built for employees of the Garden City Press), Westholm and Birds Hill. In 1907 GC Tenants built the Pixmore Estate (incorporating Pixmore Avenue, Pix Road, Broughton Hill and Ridge Road). All of this provided much needed accommodation and cottages were occupied as soon as they were finished.

Development of the Glebe Estate, comprising cottages on Common View, North Avenue and Glebe Road, began in 1907, starting with Common View on behalf of Letchworth Cottages and Buildings Ltd and then later the Howard Cottage Association from 1911 onward. A buildings study conducted by Meryvn Miller for Letchworth Garden City Heritage Foundation in 2009 refers to the Glebe Estate as being designed as a working-class neighbourhood to provide homes for factory workers. As such it was similar to the Birds Hill and Pixmore Estate south of Works Road. Together these areas of early garden city housing are an important part of Letchworth's industrial heritage, as they were specifically designed for factory workers and labourers. Using Company survey data, local Letchworth Directories and national Census records it is possible to build up a good picture of who lived in these cottages. The occupations mirror the concentrations of industries active at the time.

A locally run survey of the inhabitants of cottages in Letchworth, which was reported in newspapers in February 1906, gives a snapshot of residents' professions at the time, illustrating the lack of factory workers.

"New residents in 134 houses of the Letchworth Garden City have been thus established:-"

Professional men	19
Managers, clerks, etc.	24
Contractors and master builders	14
Farmers and small holders	8
Tradespeople	4
Hotel and lodging-house keepers	8
Artisans	59
Labourers	27
Domestic helps	25
Dressmakers etc.	2
Other occupations and not known	26
Wives, grown daughters and widows	120
Retired men and women of no occupation	19
Children of school age and under	184

By 1909 more provision had been made for workers through the efforts of the Cottage Societies. A survey of residents carried out in late 1908/early 1909 reflects this, with many labourers and workers linked to the new industries living in cottages built by these organisations. Below is an overview of the different kinds of professions listed for some of the residents of cottages built by the various societies for workers:

Birds Hill	Ridge Road	Pixmore Avenue	Pix Road
Labourer	Charwoman	Labourer	Clerk
Engineer	Accountant	Motor Engineer	Machinist
Iron Founder	Bookbinder	Machine Minder	Engineer
Moulder	Plasterer	Porter	Printer
Machinist	Carpenter	Carman	Factory Hand
Printer	Blacksmith	Gardener	Store Keeper
Foreman	Guilder	Factory Hand	House Keeper
Compositor	Milkman	Nurse	Carpenter
Packer	Printer	School Master	Caretaker
Turner	Compositor		Plasterer
Bricklayer	Pensioner		Manager
Riveter	Printer		Foreman
Carpenter	Electrician		Bookbinder
Painter	Gardener		Labourer
Blacksmith			Bricklayer
Bookbinder			Police Sergeant
Mechanic			Packer
			Compositor
			Warehouseman
			Greengrocer

Glebe Road	Westholm	Eastholm	Common View
Station Master	Carpenter	Printer	Carpenter
Clerk	Caretaker	Clerk	Labourer
Foreman	Independent means	Officer in	Bricklayer
Mineral Water	Teacher	HM Customs	Plasterer
Manufacturer	Bailiff	Bookbinder	Blacksmith
Carpenter	Ironmonger	Journalist	Boot Repairer
Painter	Builder	School Master	
Brick Layer	Potter	Independent means	
Joiner	Artist	Gardener	
Labourer	Printer	Manager	
Butcher	Postman		
Fitter	Milkman		
Clerk – weighman			

This emphasis on housing for the working classes by the Cottage Societies was very necessary in the absence of any large-scale municipal cottage building which did not start for another ten years (with the formation of Hitchin Rural District Council). There were also other smaller cottage societies active in the town but the Howard Cottage Association was not established until 1911, taking over from Letchworth Cottages and Buildings.

Post First World War developments included Burnell Rise and Campers Road (which predates the rest of the Westbury estate). This was started by the Howard Cottage Society in 1915 and built specifically to house munitions workers of the Kryn & Lahy foundry, as a result of which the area became known as "Little Belgium". Later development of the main Westbury estate – made up of Campers Road, Campers Avenue, West Avenue and High Avenue – was undertaken by Hitchin Rural District Council and Letchworth Urban District Council from 1919.

Why Letchworth lacked licensed premises

The reason the garden city had no pubs is often claimed to be because Letchworth was conceived as a "Quaker town". This is not correct and the true reason appears to be much more practical and linked to the fact that Letchworth Garden City was established as a new industrial town. It was to ensure optimum conditions for manufacturers, including the efficiency of their workforce.

A number of the manufacturers who came stated that the lack of pubs meant their men were much more effective, healthy and had a better overall quality of life. In February 1915 an article on "The Garden City and the Manufacturer", published in the *Garden Cities and Town Planning Magazine*, featured an interview with Mr. Van Hooydonk, managing director of Phoenix Motors, in which he said:

> *One great factor, I am sure, is the absence of public-houses about the industrial area, and to the manufacturer the advantage of this cannot be over-estimated. The men start out from their homes with the best will in the world, but when they have to pass a score of public-houses, it is hardly any wonder that they fall by the way.*

When asked if he was a tee-totaller, Van Hooydonk replied that he wasn't by any means but he added that the men worked so much better in the absence of public houses. He was also asked if the men themselves objected. On this he said:

> *No. I am in close touch with my own men and their families, and we have often spoken on the subject. Nine out of ten of those who are not teetotallers are opposed to having a public-house in the town. There are of course two or three on the outskirts if a man likes a stroll out after a day's work. You only have to notice the difference in the men and in their families since they have been here to see what is the result. I have some men in my factory who in London lived in, say two rooms on a back second floor, but since they have come to Letchworth they have got together quite decent homes for themselves and gardens of which anyone might be proud. I am quite convinced this town would not have progressed so well as it has done and would not have been the place it is, and the men, women, and children would not have been the people they are, if there had been a public house here.*

Van Hooydonk went on to comment on the appearance of children coming out of elementary school at Letchworth in contrast with that of the same class of child in any London district or Coventry. This testimony underlines the benefits of living in Letchworth and how quickly people noticed a difference.

An article published in the *Alliance and Temperance Review* three years earlier, in 1912, by Alexander Thompson, sheds further light on this matter. This referred to the men at first being discontented that there were no drinking establishments at the gates of their factory. It goes on to quote non-abstaining workmen who, when they first came to Letchworth, were in favour of a public house but who on polling day (for the temperance vote) campaigned and voted against it. Another man quoted was a skilled mechanic who would only take a temporary job at the motor works but who after a few weeks at Letchworth applied to be put on a permanent list.

He found that although his wages were not high he was actually much better off as he was not wasting a large part of his money in the pub.

The question as to whether to allow licensed premises in the town was put to a public vote on more than one occasion over the early years. C B Purdom wrote in his book, *The Garden City* (1913), that in 1907 voting papers were issued to every householder (man or woman) and in the case of married households to every man and woman. Lodgers were also eligible to vote as long as they had been resident in the town since Christmas Day 1906. The results of this vote were 631 against and 544 for, giving a majority of 87. Further votes took place in 1908 and 1912 and again the majority votes were against licensed premises. The 1912 poll is interesting, with results of 1,117 against and 521 for, giving a majority of 596 against. Of those whose names were on the register to vote, 58.4 per cent of women and 68.5 per cent of men voted.

Photograph showing Mrs. Callender Moss, a prominent temperance campaigner, casting her vote in 1912. Published in The Citizen newspaper, 12 January 1912.

Health of the town

Letchworth aimed to provide a healthy town for its residents – "…*the healthiest industrial town in the world*". Statistics quoted by local GP Dr Norman MacFadyen in 1918 show a significant achievement. Infant mortality in Letchworth for 1917 was 36 deaths per 1,000 compared to 97 for England and Wales and an average of 130 in other industrial districts. At the time it was claimed that 30 was about as low as could be achieved, so Letchworth certainly substantiated its claim. Even with problems such as overcrowding the town still delivered a remarkable improvement in public health. This was attributed to a combination of factors to do with the location, the way Letchworth was planned and the way people were able to live their lives. The evidence was real, so too the benefits experienced by manufacturers.

C B Purdom's later book, *The Building of Satellite Towns* (1925), includes a reference to one of the manufacturers at Letchworth (from an article which appeared in the Garden Cities and Town Planning Association journal in 1918) and a statement made at a meeting of the Local Authority:

In Letchworth the health of his own workpeople was so good, and the amount of time that they lost from ill-health or other causes was so small, that when he showed his books to friends running works in other towns, they did not believe him. At his own works he had had whole weeks during which, with 250 people, the loss of time had been less than three hours. If this was not caused by the influence of the garden city, what was the cause?

LETCHWORTH (Garden City. .)
IS THE
HEALTHIEST TOWN IN THE UNITED KINGDOM

The following comparative statistics compiled from the Registrar General's Annual Summary show that the manufacturing town of Letchworth has lower mortality rates than any other industrial town or district, or than some of our noted health resorts.

The Medical Officer of Health for the district in his annual report says: "Numbers of the children coming from large populous towns were anaemic, poor in physique and large numbers were suffering from adenoid growths and throat affections. This state of things is fast disappearing with the new conditions under which they live".

COMPARATIVE MORTALITY
Rates for 1912

TOWN	Infantile Mortality Rate per 1,000 Births	Ordinary Death Rate per 1,000
LETCHWORTH	**50.6**	**6.1**
BOURNEMOUTH	70.0	9.9
BURNLEY	145.0	14.7
HARTLEPOOL	104.0	14.5
MIDDLESBROUGH	125.0	17.2
LIVERPOOL	125.0	18.1
STOCKPORT	107.0	14.6
LONDON	101.0	13.6
STEPNEY	105.0	15.2
SHOREDITCH	123.0	18.1
HAMMERSMITH	90.0	13.1
FINSBURY	114.0	18.8
BETHNAL GREEN	96.0	15.3
POPLAR	107.0	16.4
BERMONDSEY	111.0	16.8
LEWISHAM	70.0	10.4
HAMPSTEAD	62.0	9.8

First Garden City, Ltd., Halton House, Holborn, London, E.C.; and Estate Office, Letchworth

UTILITIES

First Garden City Ltd Water Works

The provision of a water supply was the first priority in the new garden city and G R Strachan was appointed to develop Letchworth's scheme. Strachan designed and implemented a scheme which made provision for future growth. FGC Ltd's resident engineer Alfred Bullmore worked alongside him and, after Strachan's sudden death in 1907, Bullmore continued to manage all future expansions.

Alfred Bullmore, First Honorary Captain, Letchworth Fire Brigade, c.1905.

Except for in Hitchin, three miles away, there were no water supplies near the new garden city. The first borehole was sunk north of Baldock Road, a pumping station was erected with a suction gas-powered pumping engine and pumps and a reservoir constructed at Weston Hills with a capacity of 250,000 gallons.

By 1907, to meet increased demand (and the inclusion of Baldock in the supply), a second borehole was sunk and additional pumps added which were powered by electricity, unlike the initial gas pumps.

Further additions were made in 1912, with a third borehole sunk, which was of a larger diameter than the first two, and the reservoir capacity increased. This second reservoir had double the capacity of the first, at 500,000 gallons.

Water pumping station interior on Baldock Road showing workmen and also engineer Alfred Bullmore (far right).

The total capital outlay on the waterworks up to 1912 was £26,183 with an additional £7,000 spent on equipping the third well and providing new mains. The original pumping station building was a corrugated iron building, which was extended as additional capacity was added. An unfortunate fire in 1920 resulted in the need to rebuild part of the plant and then a brick building replaced part of the works.

Bullmore was also the first Fire Chief from 1905–1908 and then again from 1912–1917. There were a number of devastating fires amongst the garden city industries so a fire chief who understood the waterworks was no doubt valuable.

First Garden City Ltd Gas Works

Coal gas was generally known as town gas and by the 1820s almost every city and large town in Britain, as well as many in other countries, had a gas works, primarily for lighting the streets. Gas engines, the first successful internal combustion engines, were developed around 1860 and were popular for many industrial applications as they were smaller and more flexible than steam engines. By around 1900 many gas engines were being used to generate electricity in factories.

First Garden City Ltd, (water) pumping station, Baldock Road, c.1920s.

Charles Hunt,
consulting Gas Engineer
Engineer.

Letchworth Garden City was designed as a modern industrial town so the provision of gas was a natural choice for powering the new industries, rather than each factory burning coal to produce steam for power. An early aim was to make Letchworth a smoke-free town and, to achieve this, free meters, cookers and gas fires were provided to householders.

Charles Hunt was appointed to design the First Garden City Ltd Gas Works. He started in early 1905 and the works were complete and producing gas by September 1905. In planning the scheme Hunt made sufficient provision for the immediate needs of the town – for lighting, heating and motive power – and for the near future, with a plant to supply 6,000,000 cubic feet per annum. The site was designed with scope for expansion in mind and it quickly became necessary.

FGC Ltd Gas Works
under construction,
1905.

The initial plant included two beds of eight retorts (where coal was heated to generate gas), a brick and slate retort house with space for four additional beds, a gas-engine-driven exhauster, a pair of eight-foot purifiers, a station meter in a separate brick building and one gas holder of 52 feet in diameter with a 27,000 cubic feet capacity (and provision for telescoping). A telescoping gas holder provided greater provision for gas storage by way of a series of large interconnected (telescopic) cylindrical vessels, which rose and fell depending on the volume of the gas stored.

In 1906 consumption was already 5,000,000 cubic feet per annum. With the establishment of factories, that rose quickly to 12,000,000 by 1907, which led to the doubling of capacity at the plant. It is reported that there was a nail-biting time when the demand of factories during the day was such that the holder could not be filled quickly enough to cope with the night-time load.

Additions made in 1907 added a second holder of 62-ft diameter in two vessels providing additional storage capacity of 100,000 cubic feet and two more beds of six retorts each, a larger exhauster and engine. But consumption kept growing. By the end of 1908 it had risen to 22,000,000 cubic feet per annum, which meant the telescoping of the first holder and additional plant. By September 1909 consumption was up again, at 26,000,000 cubic feet per annum, requiring further extensions. The retort house was doubled in size with four new beds of eight retorts each installed. Consumption continued to increase and more additions were made in 1910/1911 and 1912, which increased storage capacity at the plant to 450,000 cubic feet.

Total capital outlay on the gas works reported in September 1912 was £38,644, with an additional £6,000 to be spent on the new holder and mains.

From the beginning the coal feedstock could be easily supplied by rail wagon via a siding direct into the gas works from the Great Northern Cambridge line and, indeed, a principal guest at the opening of the gas works on 10 October 1905 was Lesley Charles Probyn, Deputy Chairman of the Great Northern Railway Company (also a shareholder in FGC Ltd) together with several prominent officials of the railway company, who were all hoping for increased business not only in carrying coal to the gas works but also raw materials to and finished products from the new garden city industries.

The site of the Letchworth gas works is today completely occupied by a transport company.

First Garden City Ltd Electricity Power Station

Electricity was the last service to be developed, as it was still a relatively new technology at the time. Consulting Engineers Messrs O'Gorman and Cuzens Hardy were appointed in 1907 to plan the new power station, supported by FGC Ltd engineering department.

The original power station on Works Road was a single storey building. It was fitted with two horizontal suction gas engines, each of 100 horse-power, with belt-driven dynamos, switchboard and batteries. Suction gas engines produce gas by burning coal, coke, charcoal, or similar to feed into an internal combustion engine which provides turning power.

Electricity was started in 1907 from the generator in Works Road – a 500V d.c. system – supplying at first only the industrial area, through half a mile of mains, but in 1909 a cable was laid to the brand new Palace Cinema (or *Picture Palace*) in Eastcheap, one of the first purpose-built cinemas in the country, and the first building in the town centre with an electricity supply.

Additions to the plant were needed, and included a 220- h.p. diesel engine, and another 420-h.p. engine which led to enlargement of the power station. Further additions were a third bay filled with additional engines of 240, 350 and 500 h.p. A fourth bay was added inside and similarly filled, and outside a mass of accessory plant.

FGC Ltd Power Station c.1905 and later addition of steam powered plant in 1916.

Total capital outlay on the electricity undertaking reported in September 1912 was £20,983 and further investment followed. After a visit to Letchworth in 1916 Ewart Culpin, Secretary to the Garden City Association, wrote regularly about progress at Letchworth including about the power station growth and *"that all the engines there should have to be sufficient to meet the needs of Letchworth for some years."*

But then *"a new 1,300 horse-power multicellular Fraser and Chalmers steam turbo plant driven by Babcock & Wilcox boilers and condensers was added"* and room was left for erection of three others in same building. Outside that building a cooling tower, water softening plant, railway siding and oil storage tanks were also completed. Culpin said that 8,000 tonnes of coal were required a year to service the steam plant and providing this added to the complexity of operation. Ewart Culpin was impressed with the rate of growth and that the new steam plant had been added in just six months. He also made a comparison with Hitchin with an output of around 100,000 units per annum whereas in Letchworth output was 6,000,000. Culpin said *"like Oliver Twist manufacturers are asking for more"*.

Section Two
THE INDUSTRIES

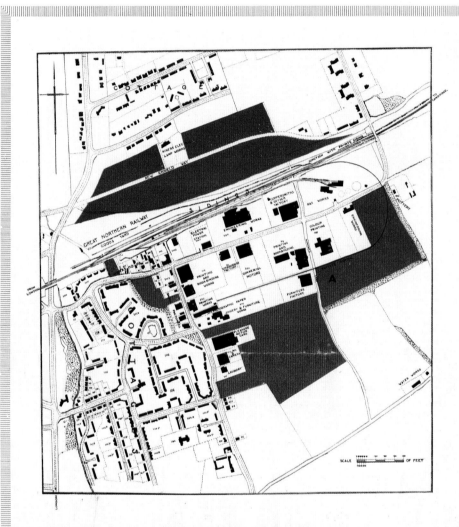

FACTORY SITES AT LETCHWORTH

THE area coloured red shows part of the factory sites offered at Letchworth. These sites will be divided up to suit the convenience of prospective tenants. They will be let on lease at low Ground Rents for 99 or 999 years. They adjoin the railway and are close to the workmen's cottages. The Garden City Company provides every facility for the erection of factories and will answer any inquiries with promptitude. Complete information will gladly be supplied if you will address, First Garden City Limited, Letchworth, Herts.

8

Extract from The Only New Industrial Town in England, a brochure produced by First Garden City to promote the industrial town of Letchworth. (1913).

PRINTING, BINDING, AND PUBLISHING IN THE GARDEN CITY

A Manufacturer's Experience of Letchworth.

Interview with Mr J.M. Dent (July 1909).

"QUITE SATISFIED" WITH GARDEN CITY AS A MANUFACTURING DISTRICT.

A Representative of "The Bookseller" recently called upon Mr J. M. Dent, or Messrs J.M. Dent & Co, the world-famed publishers of "Everyman's Library", and interviewed him respecting the causes which led to the firm removing their works from London to Garden City. The interviewer having asked for particulars of the enterprise, and how it came about, Mr Dent replied as follows: -

"That is not a very easy thing to do. I can only say that I had been for a long time discontented with the conditions under which manufacturing work, such as bookbinding, always has to be carried out in London. When, therefore, the Garden City promoters seemed to have placed their scheme on a practical business footing, I thought it offered something like the alternative of which I was in search, and after going into the thing thoroughly I determined to make the experiment and transfer my works to the new Garden City. "

"And generally speaking, are you satisfied with the result?"

"Quite satisfied; so much that I have now transferred the entire binding works to Letchworth. We have commenced printing, and next spring we intend to build model printing works, which will be thoroughly equipped and up to date. I have leased about five acres of ground, of which half is to be devoted to recreation ground and half to buildings."

"I suppose the ground rent you have to pay is a good deal less than it would be in the city?"

"Very much so. Indeed, the ground rent is only £10 per acre, and this allows me to put up buildings with only one storey – and to give our three hundred workpeople conditions of light and air and space which in London would be quite impracticable."

"And how long have you been at Letchworth?"

"We have been actively working there about two years. At first, of course, there were difficulties. We had to collect girls from the farms and villages around and had to teach them the business. Some twelve girls or so went down from London as pioneers, and now most of the girls know what they have to do, and all the workpeople are very keen to enjoy the advantages which Letchworth has to offer them. The cottages are close by, and there is already a gardeners' club of fifty men and ten women, who have decided to have an annual show, which is fixed for July 24, and for which there will be some keen competition. We have also gained the swimming trophy for the district, and in football our team beat that of Messrs. W. H. Smith & Son, and next season will perhaps do even better."

"And with your three hundred workpeople, what is your average weekly output?"

"I think about 40,000 books bound in cloth or leather. Sometimes, when pressed, we have turned out 60,000 in the week, but we only have overtime very rarely indeed, when it cannot possibly be avoided. I am particularly glad that our people have never yet lost any time. They have always been kept fully at work, though sometimes, as you can understand, it has not always been easy to do this".

At the turn of the twentieth century, printing and publishing were fast-growing industries. Techniques of mass production had brought the price of books and printing down and the improved transport network enabled speedier, more efficient distribution. For Letchworth this timing was fortuitous and with the establishment of the five main printing firms by 1907 came a rapid increase in the population.

Garden City Press, print room

Garden City Press, typesetting room

Garden City Press Ltd

The Garden City Press Ltd (GCP) was the first printing firm and industry established in connection with the new garden city, having set up in temporary premises in Bancroft, Hitchin, around November 1903. They started producing a newspaper bearing their name in 1904, which promoted the new garden city, providing news and local advertising. A section was devoted specifically to updates on the progress of the town. From such humble beginnings they quickly grew into a thriving printing operation, and began operating from premises in Letchworth two years later. The newspaper they produced ceased production when they moved. Bert Williams, the manager of GCP, left Leicester to help establish this new co-partnership printing enterprise. Employees were paid by shares in the profits and not by wages. Williams was an early and avid supporter of the garden city movement and had helped Ebenezer Howard with its promotion amongst the wider co-operative movement. The business was run as a co-partnership enterprise for over 12 years but not beyond 1917 (possibly due to the majority of its partners having been called up for war service). It was later reorganised on a limited liability basis and remained a significant employer in the town. They mainly dealt in magazines, brochures, programmes and catalogues and provided printing services to First Garden City Ltd.

Wheeler, Odell & Co

Other early printers in the town were Wheeler, Odell & Co (later Letchworth Printers Ltd), who published *The Citizen* newspaper and then specialised in the production of catalogues and booklets for London business houses. Leonard Wheeler and Harry Odell initially worked for Garden City Press but left after taking part in a union-sanctioned strike in early summer 1906. They, together with Arthur Brunt, decided to come together to produce a newspaper for the town and started up Wheeler, Odell & Co, registered on 1 August 1906. The business initially operated from Green Lane in the house occupied by Mr. Wheeler and their first *Letchworth Magazine* was published in August 1906 (edited by Charles Purdom and Fred Cole) The following month, on 22 September 1906, the first edition of *The Citizen* was published, edited by W Knight. The company moved to purpose-built premises on Norton Way North a month later.

These two printing enterprises led the way and were swiftly followed by J. M. Dent and Sons and W. H. Smith & Son (together with the Arden Press) who signed their leases on land in Letchworth in summer 1906 and began the building of their new bookbinding and printing works soon after. These later firms were attracted to the town for practical reasons – because they needed to expand; they would be operating on one level and the ground rents and low rates were moderate. Proximity to London and housing conditions for families were equally important.

C B Purdom stated in his book *The Garden City* that *"the entire success of the Garden City depends upon the extent to which it can be made a place of business"*. But even by the end of 1912 there were over 30 different factories and workshops operating in Letchworth.

J. M. Dent & Sons

The real coup for the garden city was undoubtedly the decision made by J. M. Dent & Sons in 1906 to move their bookbinding department there from Bishopsgate in London. An article in the *GCA* journal states they had been on the lookout for new premises after the success of their latest venture, the Everyman's Library, and Dent had been won over having heard Thomas Adams speak. Another strong prompt was the significantly lower cost to lease the five acres of land at Letchworth; Dent said it *"… would cost fifty times the cost to lease that amount of land in London"* as well as the much better living and working conditions on offer for his workers.

Advertisement for Wheeler, Odell & Co printers, showing their distinctive building frontage. The second image shows their location part way along Norton Way North, now demolished.

On 18 August 1906, a train was hired for the workforce and their families for a full day's visit to Letchworth. The programme included a choice of tours around the town, inspection of factory sites, viewing of some workers' cottages, and tea with musical entertainment at the end. It also included a ceremony for cutting the first sod at the site for the new factory, the contractors for which were Messrs Gilbert, Thompson & Co of Birmingham. The response from that day proved to be positive; their new premises in Dunhams Lane were completed in March 1907. Initially they operated from temporary premises, renting one of the Sheds on

J. M. Dent & Co, bookbinding works, c.1907.

Nevells Road, in which a temporary gas-engine bookbinding plant was installed at the end of 1906. Here skilled operatives from London helped train up workers in readiness for the new works. One hundred and fifty employees moved in once the new works were completed. New housing was also built in Temple Gardens, although mainly for senior employees.

It was to be a happy relationship with the town which lasted over half a century. However, Dent did threaten to pull out of the deal over delays in approval of his plans for the housing at Temple Gardens. On 4 March 1907 he wrote to Herbert Warren, FGC Ltd's solicitor *"… I really want to get this matter settled as my men are wanting their houses."* The delays appear to have been due to concerns about the drainage for the cottages. Dent tried to get approval whilst the drainage was still under further discussion so he could get started with the construction. In his letter he threatened *"If they [the Committee] will not leave me free, then I must merely cancel the business and build outside this place, which I do not want to do"*. Dent ended his letter saying he had waited too long and felt he had been very badly used. Given that his factory at Letchworth was structurally complete by this stage, he had already invested a significant amount. Clearly, this was resolved in the end but it is likely that there were delays and backlogs as the Company staff and solicitors would have been dealing with a huge number of lease negotiations and other enquiries across the estate.

Dent initially built the new binding works but leased additional land at the same time to allow for expansion and building of print works too. He said he would have liked to transfer his entire staff *"holus bolus"* if it had been practical to do so but spoke of the problems and disruption to his workers and their families with strong ties to London. Instead he moved part of his workforce, those willing to move, and built on this initial transfer over the following years.

An interesting article by C F Townsend in *Letchworth Magazine*, February 1907, criticised Dent for paying his girls who did binding *"half a living wage"* and expecting Garden City citizens to subsidise them in some way. *"An industry which cannot afford to pay a living wage to its workers has no right to exist anywhere, least of all in Garden City."*

By summer 1909 Dent employed around 300 people turning out an average weekly output of 40,000 books bound in cloth and leather; at times this output reached 60,000 books a week.

J. M. Dent & Co bookbinding works – notice how light the works are.

Frontispiece and title page to Everyman's Library volume No 766, 1925.

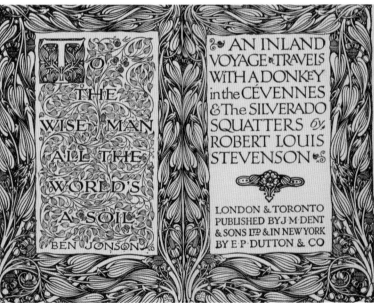

J. M. Dent was best known for publishing the Everyman's Library, early pocket-sized books of classic literature. The very first title, published in 1906, was Boswell's *Life of Johnson* and the thousandth volume in 1956 was to be Aristotle's *Metaphysics*. Dent was determined to publish new hardcovers editions of world classics at one shilling a volume, affordable to every man and woman, ensuring *"he might be intellectually rich for life"*. They would always be introduced by scholars or experts in the subject and would visually follow the design principles established by William Morris' Kelmscott Press. The books were then dispatched from Letchworth to all corners of the world and the town thus became truly the Everyman's Town.

The following words were printed in every single book:

> *Everyman, I will go with thee, and be thy guide;*
> *In thy most need to go by thy side.*

Dent and his family were concerned with the welfare and social conditions of their workforce. Just as in the Spirella factory later on, there was a works library, a gardening club, different sports fixtures were important and, of course, the annual firm's party at which the Dents themselves were always present.

Having left school himself at thirteen, Dent was a true Victorian autodidact from a Darlington house-painter family. His sons Hugh and Jack carried on the business, assisted by one of his grandsons. The family played an important role in the social, as well as the business, life of the town and made their mark here in numerous different spheres.

W. H. Smith & Son and the Arden Press 1907–1915

W. H. Smith & Son, interior views.

The corner of Works Road and Pixmore Avenue became another hive of printing once W. H. Smith & Son from Drury Lane in London, together with the Arden Press of Leamington Spa, moved into Letchworth in 1907. In 1908, W. H. Smith & Son acquired control of the Arden Press.

Mervyn Miller states in his book *Letchworth: The First Garden City* that W. H. Smith & Son signed their lease at the end of September 1906 and both firms constructed impressive single-storey works; Arden Press even built a separate cottage for their manager. The architect Francis William Troop (1859–1941) designed the factory building for W. H. Smith & Son; he was also responsible for one of the prize-winning wooden cottages for the 1905 Cheap Cottages Exhibition.

Smith's retail and bookselling arm had grown rapidly and they were looking to build up their printing and bookbinding business. Easy connections to London were needed, either by rail or road, as they dispatched books all over the world, and Letchworth fitted the bill. One hundred and fifty employees moved with Smiths and 30 with the Arden Press.

Mr. C H St John Hornby (Senior Partner, W. H. Smith & Son) said in 1907:

I can fairly say that, after working over a year, we are absolutely satisfied with having come here. We do not feel that any place in England would have suited us so well, or given us such facilities as this place has given us.

Five years later (1913) he said: *And my firm have had no reason to change their opinion with regard to Letchworth as a site for industrial purposes.*

Together with J. M. Dent and W. H. Smith & Son,, the Arden Press created a community of world-class artists in the town. Douglas Cockerell, Bernard Newdigate and Eleni Zompolides were all remarkably talented craftworkers, influenced by William Morris and his Kelmscott Press, representing some of the finest Arts & Crafts workmanship. One could indeed call it the golden period of creativity in Letchworth. Amongst the masterpieces produced at the press were *The Gold and Silver of Windsor Castle, The Objects of Art in the Collection of the Baroness James de Rothschild* and *The Collected Works of William Morris.*

Douglas Cockerell became best-known for his binding of the *Codex Sinaiticus* for the British Museum; Bernard Newdigate was at the time the country's most eminent typographer, printer and scholar, who frequently worked together with Eric Gill, the sculptor. And there was Eleni Zompolides, designer and calligrapher (who is recorded as living at 69 Norton Road in the 1912 Letchworth Directory). Their work led to the great renaissance of the lettering arts in England, as well as on the Continent.

The Letchworth this group lived in was a young and vigorous town whose founders, architects and citizens were all full of practical idealism. With the support of Dents and Arden Press these artists were able to keep to their high standards and achieve their objectives.

And, once again, the proximity to London proved to be all-important, as the company were pioneer users of road transport to their headquarters in the capital. All W. H. Smith & Son's buildings were taken over by the Ministry of Munitions during the First World War (and after that by Westinghouse Morse Chain Company) and the Company returned to London. Today, the binding works and printing works for W. H. Smith & Son and the Arden Press are the only remaining buildings from Letchworth's printing pioneers.

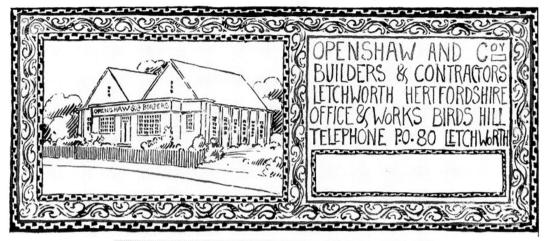

AT THE ARDEN PRESS, LETCHWORTH, is done the finest letterpress printing at quite moderate cost. Books & pamphlets well and carefully printed. The

bold simple setting of the Arden Press, Letchworth, gives clear & attractive display to advertising & commercial work.

Hayes Printing Machinery Company Ltd

Hayes Printing Machinery Company Ltd moved to Letchworth in 1911 and pioneered colour lithography, a new process invented by Mr. Jefferson Hayes. They built a significant factory located opposite the gas works on the corner of Dunhams Lane. Unfortunately, in 1913 their factory was destroyed by fire and although it was rebuilt (a condition of the lease with FGC Ltd) Hayes did not return to Letchworth. The site was later occupied by the Garden City Rubber Company (formerly the Letchworth Rubber Company). The vacated Hayes Factory was also used to house Belgian refugees during the war.

The fine premises built for the Hayes Printing Machinery Co Ltd prior to the devastating fire.

MOTOR INDUSTRY
IN LETCHWORTH

Lacre Motor Car Company Ltd. advertisement, c. May 1921 (Source: Grace's Guide)

The early years

Letchworth Garden City was founded in 1903, which was about a decade after the start of the motor industry in Britain. A number of expanding motor car manufacturers joined other industrial pioneers, moving to the new garden city in its first decade.

Lacre Motor Car Company Ltd

In August 1909 Lacre was the first manufacturer to build motor vehicles in Letchworth.

The Long Acre Car Company was formed by Claude Browne in January 1902 at Long Acre, Covent Garden, hence its name. The company's address was changed to Poland Street in 1903 and its name shortened to Lacre, establishing a name associated with the motor industry to this day. In 1904 its first van was built, with a payload of 25cwt. and fitted with a 16 h.p. engine, which was used in all early Lacre vans irrespective of size. Orders began to flow into the company after businesses were convinced that vans were a more cost-effective proposition than horse-drawn vehicles and the range of commercial vehicles was expanded to meet this demand.

For a while before 1909 Claude Browne had been concerned that production demands were going to outstrip the available space at Poland Street and, after much deliberation, in 1909 a new factory was built in Works Road, Letchworth. The building was carefully planned with bright, well-ventilated and heated working conditions for the staff, which eventually numbered over 300. The company claimed at the time that theirs was the first factory in the country to be specially designed and built for the manufacture of commercial motor vehicles. The latest equipment was installed and by the outbreak of war in 1914 the Letchworth factory was producing nineteen models, which maintained an enviable reputation for workmanship and reliability. Commercial vehicle production completely outstripped that of cars at quite an early stage and after about 1912 Lacre-built cars could no longer be obtained.

In 1909 the Lacre Motor Car Co. was an important company which had a very large business in commercial motor cars of the very first repute. This company was hoping to employ, almost immediately, from 50 to 100 people at Letchworth. They were a very efficient and energetic firm and they had considered the advantages of Letchworth, both from the business point of view and from the point of view of the wellbeing of their workers. Among the reasons they

Lacre Motor Car Company Ltd; workers from the fitting department outside the Pixmore Institute.

61

gave for coming to Letchworth were that they could get electrical power more cheaply than they could produce themselves, and the strong influences they felt to be behind the whole project. The factory was hardly complete yet, but, such was the demand for their cars, they were already beginning to talk of the necessity of extending it.

In the new factory a new series of commercial models was introduced, ranging from 10cwt. to 5 tons payload, and most of the component parts were made on site. Four engines between 15 and 38 h.p. were fitted, depending on load capacity. Various chassis were fitted to Lacres, including open and closed lorries and vans, buses and a twelve-seater charabanc.

About the same time, a new sales office and maintenance department was opened at 78 York Road, near Kings Cross Station.

The wellbeing of their employees was important; for example, a train was hired for a holiday excursion to Great Yarmouth in August 1911.

War brought heavy demands on the company. Lacre lorries received compliments from the Belgian Army who purchased the entire output for the first two years of the war after an initial order had been delivered on time in 1914. The company's Chief Engineer, James Sidney Drewry, who joined Lacre in 1911, was decorated by the Belgian Government for his work in designing and building unique pontoon equipment for the Belgian Army. He also produced special equipment for the British Forces. He left Lacre in 1922 to design a special type of low-loading freighter and became co-founder of Shelvoke and Drewry Ltd with Harry Shelvoke, who was manager at Lacre at the time.

Their best-known model was the O-Type, which had a two–three ton payload and 30 h.p. engines. Several hundred were built during and after the First World War, to be used as vans, buses, Black Marias, tippers, ambulances and estate cars.

Unfortunately, the war left a serious trade depression in its wake which lasted well into the 1920s. During this time many vehicle builders fell on hard times as prices and demand dropped and the market was flooded with reconditioned ex-war vehicles at almost give-away prices, including Lacres.

Fortunately, Lacre had realised early the value of municipal orders, particularly for specialised vehicles such as refuse collectors and road sweepers. These were first

Particulars and Plan of

A VALUABLE LONG LEASEHOLD

GROUND FLOOR FACTORY
LETCHWORTH

HERTFORDSHIRE

CONTAINING A

FLOOR SPACE OF **48,500** SQUARE FEET

including an imposing Two-Storey Office Building

AND COVERING A

SITE AREA OF 3½ ACRES

For further particulars, apply—

FIRST GARDEN CITY LTD.

ESTATE OFFICE, LETCHWORTH

HERTS

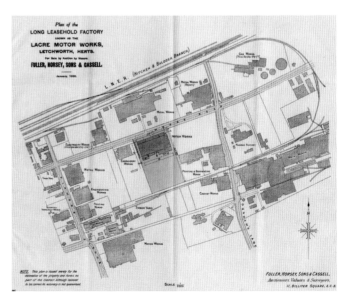

built in 1917 and, although it could not be seen at the time, this development was to be the saviour of the company in the lean times that were to follow as the market for other vehicles contracted. In 1919, when the market for municipal vehicles was expanding, Lacre began producing L-Type road sweepers and refuse collectors, which continued for over twenty years.

In 1936 Lacre transferred their operation to Welwyn Garden City and later to St. Albans in 1959.

Phoenix Motor Company

In 1910, a year after Lacre had had their new factory built in Works Road, the Phoenix Motor Company from North London established themselves in Pixmore Avenue.

Phoenix Motor Cycle Works was founded by Brussels-born Mr. Joseph Van Hooydonk and had its origins as a cycle business in Holloway Road, London, in 1900. A tri-car was developed, on which a passenger sat between two front steerable wheels with the rider (driver) mounted behind and the rear wheel was driven by a single cylinder engine. These early tri-cars were inherently unstable, however, and a more complicated and robust version, called the Trimo, was developed, which used a horizontal sub-frame.

In 1904, the company moved to Blundell Street, Caledonian Road, North London and became a limited company, Phoenix Motors Ltd, with Mr. J Van Hooydonk and Mr. A F Ilsley as joint Managing Directors. Production of Trimos continued, with customers having a choice of $2^{3}/_{4}$ h.p. or $3^{1}/_{2}$ h.p. engines.

A few years later the works in North London became too small and it was too expensive to remain there and extend. Mr. Van Hooydonk considered Letchworth or Coventry as alternative business sites. At the latter there was a factory vacant which he could rent straight away; at Letchworth he had to take two acres of ground and build one. In the end he decided on Letchworth and never regretted his decision. He was more than satisfied with the move and believed it had been an enormous financial advantage for his firm. The fact that Letchworth was 34 miles from London was, in his opinion, no hindrance whatsoever, and the advantages were so enormous, rent and rates being about half the costs in Letchworth for larger plots.

Phoenix Motor Works, c.1909/10.

He brought with him about 40 of the men who had been working with him in London, recruited more locally, and, although a few returned, the majority remained in Letchworth. In February 1915 an article, "The Garden City and the Manufacturer", published in the *Garden Cities and Town Planning* magazine, featured an interview with Mr. Van Hooydonk. When asked as to the effect upon the work and physique of the men he replied:

> *When I was told first of all, that the result of bringing men to Letchworth would be that they would work better, I looked upon it as one of those fairy tales which are always held out to induce people to come to one place or another, but it was not so I can prove. I brought down my own men, tools and material, and the same work was done in Letchworth as London, with the result that the men are turning out more work and earning more money making exactly the same car. A man working on a lathe at Letchworth will do more work than the same man working on the same lathe in London.*

> *Another thing is that Letchworth, with the advantages of a factory built on the most modern principles, all on one floor, open all round, and with a perfect north light, there is practically no necessity for artificial light except just in the darkest days of the year. In the case of the Phoenix works, they started at Letchworth with a building 120 by 130 feet but was later increased to more than 240 by 130 feet, with a paint room at the end and other departments at the sides. This indicates a considerable increase in business, the staff of sixty at the beginning having grown to two hundred, while there is an acre of land at the side for future building. Besides this, there is a recreation ground belonging to the various sports clubs run in connection with the firm, and the men and their wives seem to take a keen interest in the place.*

Mr. Van Hooydonk laid great stress upon that point – that the *"spirit of the place"* seemed to have got into the factories also, and there was an absence of callousness on the part of the men. They seemed to be proud of their firm, and to take a pride in all that concerned it.

> *Regular timekeeping, which is so necessary in the commercial world, is obtainable in Letchworth, with the difference in loss of time at Letchworth and at London being enormous. As a matter of fact, at Phoenix there is scarcely any loss of time.*

Asked his reasons, Mr. Van Hooydonk said, "f*or one thing, I attribute it to the men living reasonably near to the factory."* He also believed strongly that the absence of public houses in Letchworth was beneficial to manufacturers.

One of the men who, along with his family, had been living and working in Coventry, said that they were all better in health and physique and were enjoying life better. He had a house with four bedrooms and three downstairs rooms for 10s a week, which would cost him 16s or 18s a week in Coventry, and he had a good garden besides.

Mr. Van Hooydonk said that he knew very little about the garden city idea but was very interested from the development point of view, with the advantage of a defined factory area in the town being separated from the residential area. It was the garden city ideal about which, at first, he was sceptical. *"Since then"* he said, *"I have seen it at work and got an insight into it, and it appeals to me. I think there is good work being done, and what is being done is giving the men a chance. A man in the big town does not get a chance, and as for the children – well, it is quite enough to look for yourselves."*

Together with Mr. A E Bowyer-Lowe, who joined the company in 1905 as a designer, Van Hooydonk developed an 8/10 h.p. quad-car. However, it was not until the company moved to Letchworth in 1910 that a four-cylinder engine (the first engine of its own manufacture) car was offered with prices starting from £230. In 1912 Phoenix exhibited their new 11.9 h.p. four-cylinder engine car at the Olympia Motor Show and it was well received. The cars were built at the rate of about seven a week in batches of 25, with the factory employing about 150 operatives. This turned out to be their most successful model by far and although a six-cylinder 17.9 h.p. car was also offered this turned out not to be such a commercial success.

Some Views in the Phœnix Works, Letchworth.

Image accompanying an article and interview with Mr. J Van Hooydonk, published in the Garden Cities and Town Planning journal February 1915.

Production of the four-cylinder car continued until 1922 when it was dropped in favour of a 12/25 Meadows-engined car.

In addition to making use of commercially available machine tools, Phoenix, probably under the stewardship of Bowyer-Lowe, also designed its own equipment and accessories. Prior to fitting in the cars, every engine was run on the bench, at first by town gas, then on petrol, with horse-power readings taken electrically. Road tests were made under the stewardship of the head tester, George Howell.

A London depot at Whitcher Place in Camden Town was maintained as a repair facility only and a showroom was opened at 114 Great Portland Street.

During this time the company was employing around 200 staff and building about 400 cars each year. With their high ground-clearance, the car was much in demand in India and Africa and was exported there in great numbers.

During the First World War, Phoenix, like other engineering companies, changed over to munitions work.

The year 1928 was the last in which Phoenix cars were manufactured in Letchworth and the first year the Ascot Motor Company started its operation on the site.

The Phoenix Motor Works was recently redeveloped and is now a residential area called Phoenix Park, only the front of the building remaining.

Warne / Pearsall-Warne Ltd

In late 1912 the Warne Motor Co. Ltd started building a small, light, four-wheeled cyclecar in Icknield Way, Letchworth. Their main showroom was located at 152 Shaftesbury Avenue, London.

Warne Motor Co. Ltd advertisement from 1912 (Source: Grace's Guide).

The car had a lightweight two-seat open body with a convertible top and was powered by an eight h.p. 964cc V-twin engine from the John A. Prestwich Company. This was increased to 1,070cc in 1915. Drive was to the rear wheels by belts for weight reasons. Although air-cooled, the car was given a conventional appearance by fitting a dummy radiator.

By 1913 the company was manufacturing six cars a week and they were sold for the modest price of £99. Warne may not have had a lot of success, but they were renowned for their quality and this probably led to the cars being popular with the rallying community. Unfortunately, in 1915, the war curtailed any further increase in motor vehicles being produced in Letchworth and led to the demise of the Warne motor business.

In the London "Evening News," Mr. John Phillimore says in regard to the running of the "WARNE CAR"—

". . . The absence of vibration, too, was marked, both at high as well as low revolution rate. I soon felt that the car was capable of good speed, and would prove a fine hill climber. This was amply proved when we tackled Brockley Hill. Without any undue 'rushing' we went up in fine style.

"THIS WAS THE BEST PERFORMANCE I HAVE YET DONE ON A CYCLECAR.

"In traffic she is all one wants, being flexible and possessing a most surprising speed in 'picking up.'"

The "WARNE" car, the TRUE cyclecar, embodies motorcycle simplicity and economy with car comfort and cleanliness. The same service can be obtained from a "WARNE" car costing under £100, as from a car costing £400, at about one-tenth the running cost.

THE
WARNE
CAR

THE WARNE CAR CO.,
152, Shaftesbury Avenue, W.C.

Tally-Ho Motor Company

In 1914 the Tally-Ho Motor Company came to Letchworth and occupied part of the Tenement building in Works Road, with Thomas Hedges as proprietor. It appears that only three cars were produced here. Almost immediately, however, the factory, now known as Tally-Ho Motors and Munitions, was altered to produce munitions for the war effort. The company continued to carry out government contracts to produce munitions during the war but owing to cessation of hostilities this work soon ceased. The company decided, in view of the scarcity of gramophone motors, that the works should be converted to produce these motors. A contract was obtained to manufacture as many motors as could be delivered, but difficulty was experienced in securing a supply of motor parts, and eventually a winding-up order prevented completion of the contract.

It is believed that the origins of Tally-Ho may have been in Australia, with Tally-Ho being a suburb of Melbourne. Insurance for the motor cars was arranged through agents F W Moore & Co., Australian Merchants. In 1917, the army reserve employed George Bell, the well-known Australian war artist, as a fitter carrying out munitions work at Tally-Ho Motors and Munitions.

FOUNDRIES AND OTHER ENGINEERING MANUFACTURERS

Contemporary trade advertisement published during their early years in Letchworth.

Kryn & Lahy

The beginnings – forged in war

On 26 July 1915 a refugee from the advancing German Army in Belgium wrote to his sister in his native French from the Garden City Hotel in Letchworth.

He was just one of the quarter of a million Belgian refugees in Great Britain, following the outbreak of the First World War and the German attack on Belgium on 4 August 1914. Antwerp had to be abandoned on 9 October.

Joseph Louis Gaston Deschamps wrote to *"Ma chère Lucie"* in France that he'd found here in Letchworth the situation he needed, employment as a lathe turner in a Belgian (underlined in his letter) factory, staffed entirely by Belgians, four to five hundred *"of us"*, making shells.

Lack of shells for the British Army had been a serious problem since autumn 1914 and was a major cause of a political crisis in May 1915 when Prime Minister Asquith formed a new coalition government and David Lloyd George was appointed as Minister of Munitions. So the output of this Belgian firm in Letchworth was sorely needed at this time. The Garden City Collection has their millionth shell, which was proudly presented to David Lloyd George later in the war.

Joseph Deschamps also pointed out to his sister Lucie that among the several hundred employees were fifteen or so professionals – engineers, doctors, lawyers, etc. With his engineering qualification Joseph had found it easy to get this work on a machine tool, work which interestsed him, and he stated that he was working eleven hours every day, earning *"a little more than nine francs a day"* but hoped to be getting twelve in a few weeks and fifteen in a few months.

The Belgian factory that Joseph Deschamps had come to work for was Kryn & Lahy, set up as a direct result of the German incursion into Belgium looking for an easy route to attack France. Joseph had to flee from Tournai with his wife and two tiny daughters, first to Holland, where they were given refuge by a family, and then on to Britain at the beginning of 1915. Starting at the bottom on a lathe, but obviously qualified for much higher level work, Joseph Deschamps soon progressed to General Manager, then Managing Director, and finally, while most of his compatriots returned to Belgium after the Armistice in 1918, he stayed on in the top role and died in Hertfordshire, still in service at Kryn & Lahy, in 1941.

This Belgian foundry and armaments maker was an unlikely arrival in the new industrial city of Letchworth. The earliest manufacturers after the 1903 founding of Letchworth Garden City (and let us not forget that the aim of the new city was to establish a home for industry and its workers, away from the crowded slums of the existing big cities, in an ideal mix of town and countryside) were publishers like J. M. Dent of the Temple Press and W. H. Smith & Son, a mineral-water maker, a furniture maker, and some general engineering companies making pumps, prams and early motor cars.

In October 1914, when the German army was rapidly closing in on Antwerp, one of Belgium's most prominent diamond merchants, Jacques Kryn, fled to England. With him came his younger brother, Georges, an engineer by profession and manufacturer of the Sava car, who brought with him Raoul Lahy, his works manager from the Sava factory near Brussels. The Sava vehicles had been adapted into armoured cars and so there was already some involvement in military wares. Georges Kryn also had the reputation of being the finest swordsman in Belgium, and was well known in sporting circles in Great Britain as a keen horseman and a frequent judge at international competitions.

Legend had it that Jacques Kryn arrived with his pockets stuffed with diamonds and it is said that he managed to bring roughly £1 million worth of uncut diamonds with him to London. The diamond trade was in the doldrums. He suggested to his friend, Sir Bernard Oppenheimer, a South African millionaire who had offices in the City, and with whom he had transacted a great deal of diamond business over many years, that between them they should start a works to manufacture munitions and use the services of the thousands of Belgian refugees who had fled to England.

Sir Bernard agreed to this, and production commenced on a limited scale in the empty Pearsall-Warne plant in Icknield Way, Letchworth – initially financed by Sir Bernard and one of his partners, H.Scott Dennington – in January 1915.

3,000 Belgians in Letchworth

There were some problems of perception about the million or more Belgians who had fled their country and found refuge in neutral Holland or in the combatant countries, France and Great Britain. Some of the six million who had stayed, and whose country was now occupied by the German Army, felt that those who had fled were having a much easier time than they were, and there was even a feeling that maybe the refugees were somehow betraying their homeland. Tales of atrocities committed by the German Army against Belgian civilians were widely circulated and created much sympathy in France and England for the refugees and this feeling is also evident in Letchworth where the refugees were at first warmly welcomed.

A committee had been formed in September 1914 by the residents of Letchworth Garden City to welcome Belgian refugees and a party of 37 arrived from London on 18 September, described as *"all belonging to the artisan or peasant class"* and comprising nine families and two single people. Accommodation had been found for the group within a week and a house that had been furnished by local contributions of money, clothing and furniture had been allocated to one family of nine. Communication was difficult as the French managed by local Letchworth residents did not seem to be well understood by the new arrivals. Dr Adrian Fortescue, Letchworth's Catholic priest, was able to speak to some in Flemish. Some refugees were housed in empty factory premises, shops, or houses.

F Nott Bakery, Eastcheap, c.1913.

Fred Nott, a young baker who had moved from the South Coast to Letchworth in the very early days to make his fortune in the garden city, was offering his bakery products in three languages outside his Eastcheap shop. Chocolate Fingers were 1d each, matched by *Doigts au Chocolat 1d la pièce*, and *Vingers met Chocolade 1d het stuk*.

However, the arrival of many young, healthy, Belgian men in the town, not in uniform, must have upset several Letchworth residents whose own sons had already volunteered to go off to the western front in France and Belgium. The fact that thousands of these men were soon involved in heavy work at the new Kryn & Lahy foundry, producing steel for millions of shells for that front, must have helped to appease those hostile feelings.

One Belgian who died in Letchworth after working at Kryn & Lahy was Joseph Joiret. If you visit the little church of St Mary the Virgin, which has served Letchworth since Norman times, you see on your left as you enter the churchyard the tombstone dedicated to Joseph Joiret, inscribed in the French language to *"our brother and much missed friend"*, born in Châtelet on 5 May 1888, wounded at Malines on 26 August 1914, died in Letchworth 17 November 1918. Then in English is inscribed *"in Remembrance from his fellow workers of Kryn & Lahy Ml. Wks R.I.P."*

His death occurred a few days after the Armistice ended the war in which he'd received his ultimately fatal wound. His entry on the Belgian Register of War Dead says he died in *"Letchvoort (GB)"* of pneumonia and heart failure. He was married to Louise Celine Marie Rosalie but it's not clear where his wife was at the time of Joseph's death.

Joseph was just one of several wounded Belgian soldiers who found refuge at Kryn & Lahy during the First World War.

On 26 February 1915 *The Citizen* reported that its reporter had seen members of the *"Kryn & Lahy Company of Metal Workers"* at its offices in London. They were told that the company had

Workers in front of the factory.

been engaged in different engineering projects, including diamond mining, but an entirely new company was being formed now for this English venture. They expected that the range of their work would be wide, including all kinds of industry from the foundry to finished goods. They had work to go on with, and operations would commence as soon as ever the men could be assembled. As these men reached Letchworth they would be set to work. *The Citizen* journalist asked what sort of people would be coming to staff the new factory and was told that they would be both single men and men with wives and families and that *"several hundreds would be coming soon"*. The journalist worried that the quiet life in Letchworth, with the inhabitants discussing the *"riddles of life"* at home, might not be much of a substitute for the merrier café scene on the Continent but the Kryn & Lahy man assured him that *"In any case they will be happier in Letchworth than in Belgium just now."* Asked about language communication problems, the Belgian said that these people speak *"French. Not many speak Flemish. These people are Walloons."*

Contrast the planned military output of this new undertaking with the reputation of Letchworth for its smock-and-sandal-wearing residents, many of whom were resolutely opposed to the war. There were several prominent conscientious objectors, including in 1916 Herbert Morrison, later a cabinet minister in the Second World War, who worked as a labourer at a farm in Letchworth instead of going into uniform. Conscription for eighteen to 41 year olds replaced volunteering in January 1916.

Notice of the imminent arrival of the Belgian factory caused consternation among some inhabitants on aesthetic grounds, as reported in *The Citizen* of 26 February 1915: *"this caused alarm in many quarters, for it seemed to announce a definite abandonment of the policy of keeping unsightly features in the background instead of flaunting them in the face of visitors and travellers. People who know what an engineer's yard is like shuddered at the prospect..."*

Estimates of the number of Belgians who fled to Great Britain at the beginning of the First World War vary between 225,000 and 265,000. This estimation does not include the roughly 150,000 Belgian soldiers that had taken leave in Britain at some point in the war and an additional 25,000 wounded Belgian soldiers convalescing in Britain.

Ebenezer Howard himself, the founder of Letchworth Garden City, addressed *"Representatives of the brave Belgian nation"* on 15 February 1915, welcoming them to *"our little town"* and it's difficult to imagine that one or all of Jacques and Georges Kryn and Raoul Lahy were not among his audience.

On Friday 30 July 1915 the *Luton Times and Advertiser* reported:

> *The development of Letchworth is proceeding apace, but house accommodation is at a premium owing to the large influx of Belgium workers in connection with the newly established Kryn Lahy works.[sic].*

Housing was found for many families in new developments in Glebe Road and then in the Westbury estate comprising Burnell Rise, Campers Road and Campers Place, off Spring Road, and this area became known as Little Antwerp or Little Belgium.

Much later, on Thursday 4 Oct 1917, the *Luton News and Bedfordshire Chronicle* reported:

> *Overcrowding at Letchworth has assumed the most acute phase. It is said there are many houses with 10, 12, or 15 residents, and the population is increasing every day. The Kryn-Lahy works employ 2300 people and a new factory has recently been opened. It is computed that 500 houses are now required in the place, with 100 additional at the end of the war.*

There are local recollections of Kryn & Lahy: one lady remembers:, *"The Belgian man who lived with us was called Verreyt and he used to work there [Kryn & Lahy]. Sometimes he would be there for forty hours straight off working on the blast furnaces. In his own trade he was an architect at Malines in Belgium."*

Colin Clapson contributed his recollection to the Herts Memories website about Belgian refugees in Letchworth. His mother had been born in Letchworth in 1919 to Belgian parents who had fled through Ostend in 1914. *"In her nineties my grandmother still had cards with the lyrics of songs like 'Keep the Home Fires Burning' – songs she sang after a hard day's work in the munition factory in Letchworth."*

Foundry work

Work was commenced in February 1915 on a contract from Vickers, through the War Office, (this was before a Ministry of Munitions had been established) for 650,000 eighteen-pound shells.

Soon the scale of the work undertaken at the new Kryn & Lahy works outgrew the original premises in Icknield Way and a bigger 27 acre site on the east side of Dunhams Lane was acquired later in 1915, south of where the Hayes Reynold (calico printers) factory had stood, until destroyed by fire in May 1913, and next to the private siding that branched off the Great Northern Railway line to serve the garden city's industrial area. Hitchin Rural District Council gave permission for this to go ahead on 9 March 1915.

At the beginning of 1916 the foundry was installed to maximise use of the skills and techniques of the many steel foundry workers among the Belgian refugees and the machine shops were enlarged. To start with, two cupolas and a one-ton converter were built, and the foundry went into production in a small way on steel castings of various types for munitions of war, but eventually the largest output was the manufacture of tank parts. A printed account of the history of Kryn & Lahy, held by the Garden City Collection, describes work at the plant as follows:

> *Life in the foundry in the early days was an interesting experience for an Englishman, of whom for some time, there were only a few. It became necessary for him to make himself as far as possible bi-lingual, and to understand that his superiors were "brigadiers" and "chefs". Needless to say the Englishmen "murdered" the French language, just as the Walloons "murdered" English, but the Flemish were much better in picking up the English language. There was usually a strong antagonism between the Walloons and Flemish, and it often happened that in any conversation between them, neither would demean himself to speak or pretend to understand the other's language, so they resorted to English, of which at first both knew very little.*

Work in the foundry was in two shifts, 6.30 am to 6.30 pm and 6.30 pm to 6.30 am, six days a week, and till noon on Sunday. There was a break at 8.30 am until 9.00 am, and then a lunch break from 1.00 pm until 2.15 pm. Mainly men worked in the foundry and 65 separate charges of metal from the furnaces was achieved each 24 hours, making a record 1500 tons of castings one month.

While the machine shops were being enlarged, the company had been developing the Inglis Pyramid portable bridge, for use by the British Army, in conjunction with Professor Charles Edward Inglis, then head of the engineering laboratories at Cambridge University. By the end of 1916 separate shops had been erected to build these bridges, many of which were still standing after the Great War as permanent structures in Northern France.

By 1918 First Garden City's "Plan of Present Development" shows the Kryn & Lahy metal works occupying a building of a size bigger by far than any other works in the industrial area and stretching from Dunhams Lane eastwards to a point roughly where Sainsburys' petrol station now stands.

Transport

A shunting locomotive was purchased in 1917 and was much needed because on some days as many as 60 wagons were brought in by the railway company via the siding from the Great Northern line to Cambridge. Although there seem to be no existing photographs showing horses employed at the works during the Great War, horses and carts were definitely in use later to move sand in the foundry. A visitor to the Letchworth Local History Group's 2015 Exhibition celebrating the garden city's early industries told the author he remembered, as a small boy in the Second World War, the horses going down Green Lane every morning and back each evening, to and from Kryn & Lahy. Presumably they were coming from a farm in the Norton area. Also, a memory in *Letchworth Recollections* relates *"We knew the time of day by the horses coming up the road with these tip carts containing sand and gravel. They used to do a lot of work for Kryn and they would come up the road at about 4.30 pm. (Grandfather) used to do a lot of carting for Kryn because there were no lorries."*

The Inglis Portable Bridge, developed by Kryn & Lahy and Professor Charles Inglis of Cambridge University.

The children

In *The Citizen* interview with Kryn & Lahy in London, reported on 26 Feb 1916, the journalist had asked whether the children would need schools of their own or would the parents be willing to send them to the English schools. The answer to this question had been unhesitating. They would certainly go to the schools that were already in existence, and as for the language difficulty, that would disappear very soon. *"Why, in five or six months my grandchildren could speak English quite well. No, there will be no trouble about that. They will speak their own language at home, and English at school, and so they will have two languages instead of one."* Many of the children of those early refugees went on to Norton School, which had been founded in 1905. Joseph Deschamps' two little daughters, who arrived with him in Letchworth in 1915, went on to be educated at St Christopher School after the war, when it was situated in Broadway on the site now occupied by St Francis' College.

Temperance

The Citizen also pointed out that *"teetotalism is not strong on the continent"*, and asked whether the men were likely to be disappointed at finding no central public house in the garden city. *"The firm will be very happy to be without a public house, and the men who want beer will be able to walk out a little way to get it."* was the reply from Kryn & Lahy.

Interestingly, this was also the attitude of several of the employers who moved to Letchworth in those early years before the outbreak of war. They believed that their workpeople benefited greatly by not having the temptations of a public house after work but enjoyed instead life with the family at home and tending their new gardens. The refusal to allow licensed premises to open in the central part of the garden city arose from a regularly taken vote of the residents over 25 years old, men and women, this before the implementation of full female suffrage for the parliamentary elections.

Aerial view of Kryn & Lahy, 1922. Source: Grace's Guide.

After the Great War

This factory, so important for the British war effort 1914–1918, still had many years of development to come after the Armistice that ended the cataclysmic struggle. Most of the thousands of Belgians who had lived in Letchworth and laboured in the plant went home quite quickly during 1919 and 1920. The company was faced with the difficulty of reconstructing the works, which had spent almost four years devoted to making the implements of war, to enable it to deal with peacetime requirements, and also establishing the necessary connections with potential customers, such as leading railway companies and engineering firms. This occupied a great deal of time, and it took nearly two years to bring the works back into full production.

During this period Kryn & Lahy missed out on the best part of the post-war boom, and by the time the works were re-equipped the trade boom had dissipated and the years of slump were beginning. They did, though, overcome this lean period and established a fine reputation for making, especially, quality wheels and other metal castings for railway locomotives and wagons.

Our story ends here as we are restricting ourselves to the first couple of decades of Letchworth's industrial history but Kryn & Lahy went on to develop a famous *Stronger Steel*, continued as a major supplier to the railways, provided the steel for a huge project – the Kincardine Bridge over the Forth – incorporated Jones Cranes, which were exported all over the world, and survived at Letchworth until 1979, the year Mrs. Thatcher arrived as Prime Minister.

Heatly Gresham Engineering Co. Ltd

Harry Heatly and Frank Gresham leased five acres of land on Works Road in September 1904, with work beginning on the garden city's first significant factory the following May. They were linked to both Gresham and Craven of Manchester and Heatly & Gresham Ltd of London and India.

Heatly Gresham Engineering Co. Ltd was established in 1900 in Bassingbourn, near Royston. There the company made an oil engine called the Rational, which was mostly exported to India, and also pioneered some of the earliest forms of the motor car. Known as The Rationals these were the earliest taxis on London streets. Production of motor cars ceased after moving to Letchworth but they retained Rational as part of their trade mark and still made components for motor cars.

In Bassingbourn Heatly Gresham employed about twenty people but both Heatly and Gresham were ambitious and the garden city provided an ideal opportunity to expand the business as well as allowing them to site their factory on a prime plot adjacent to railway sidings. By November 1905 their new factory at Letchworth was completed and they were in operation. That month the Garden City Association wrote about the progress of industries in their quarterly journal, *The Garden City*. About Heatly Gresham they said that this new factory was in operation and would soon employ 100–150 men. They also thought that this company could become one of the most important works in the town due to the quality and demand for their products. How right they were!

Heatly Gresham Engineering works adjacent to railway siding.

Cottages built for Heatly Gresham workers, Birds Hill.

Among some of the earliest cottages approved for building were sixteen built for the Heatly Gresham workers who moved from Bassingbourn. Located at the bottom end of Birds Hill, they are affectionately referred to locally as the Noah's Ark cottages (due to their distinctive roof design). They were designed by the architect Victor Dunkerley. Originally there were 22 cottages in total built for the Letchworth Building Syndicate. A similar pair of cottages

Engineering works interior.

designed by Dunkerley were also built on Nevells Road and entered into the 1905 Cheap Cottages Exhibition. The cottages at Birds Hill (at the time known as Station Road East) for Heatly Gresham were constructed by Picton & Hope, locally based builders who advertised themselves as the *"pioneer builders"*. Interestingly, archive correspondence between the architect and the builders, dated 15 July 1905, refers to delays with the development, which the architect was not happy about. At this time work would also have been starting on the factory so there was a pressing need to ensure the accommodation would be available for their workers relocating to Letchworth. Using a local survey, the 1911 Census and Letchworth Directories, it is possible to identify where other Heatly Gresham workers most likely lived. As the factory grew, many engineers, machinists and foundry workers lived on the Pixmore and Glebe estates. Both these provided attractive and purpose-designed accommodation for workers.

Workers outside the factory.

The move to Letchworth was successful for Heatly Gresham and the company quickly expanded, almost doubling the size of their works just one year from their opening. They moved into the manufacture of a wider range of products including Rational patent oil engines, vacuum exhausters, air compressors, iron castings, steel stampings, drop forgings and railway materials, particularly component parts for the automatic continuous vacuum brake. The latter area of business brought them into direct competition with the Westinghouse Air Brake Company (who manufactured the railway air brake invented and patented by American inventor, George Westinghouse). Interestingly, another of the Westinghouse companies came to Letchworth in 1919 – The Westinghouse Morse Chain Company – setting up opposite Heatly Gresham in the former W. H. Smith & Son bookbinding works.

Grace's Guide states that, in 1915, the War Office sanctioned the Heatly Gresham *"On War Service"* badge to identify the wearer as engaged in essential war work. This included *"…supplying the petrol-driven Electric Lighting set for use on Earl Haig's train in France"*.

By the 1920s their works were a significant size as a press article, from a series published in *The Citizen*, indicates *"… some factories are practically machine shops, others are foundries and machine shops; but Heatly Gresham Engineering Company combines every detail of its manufacture from start to finish. This includes the fabrication of steel in forges and presses, and all processes in foundry, machine shop, plating and stamping departments and assembly work."* Some finishing was also carried out at the Company's associated firm in Manchester – Messrs Gresham and Craven. In Letchworth the company had extensive pattern stores and a carpenter's shop. They even had a multi-unit train available for testing of vacuum brakes on electrical rolling stock.

At its height Heatly Gresham employed over 300 men and evidence of their attention to staff welfare is that they also retained a significant number of the twenty or so men who moved from Bassingbourn to Letchworth with them and who were provided with accommodation. The Company were leaders in the Inter-Works Sports League in Letchworth (including football, cricket and billiards).

In 1933, the business was transferred to Manchester and the parent company, Heatly Gresham, seems still to operate in India (www.hgresham.com).

Lloyds & Company Letchworth Ltd

"Manufacturers of high-quality mowing equipment"

Lloyd, Lawrence & Company was founded by John Post Lawrence in 1878 as an agency for the import of the American *"Pennsylvanian"*, *"Chicago"*, and other American mowing machines. The year 2018 was Lloyds & Company Letchworth's (as they became known) 140th year in business and over 100 years at Letchworth.

Advertisement for "Planet J.R" Horse and Hand Implements and sales receipt for parts for the "Planet J.R." parts, issued by Lloyds & Co., 1919.

The company started out at 29 Worship Lane, London, *"between a public-house and a police station"*, as the Chairman, J P Lawrence described it in 1937 They found these initial premises to be inadequate, and made the decision to relocate to Letchworth in 1913. An article in *The Citizen* of 12 March 1915 announced that Openshaw and Co. had commenced building a substantial factory and separate offices for Messrs. Lloyds and Co. at the summit of Birds Hill, the design and supervision of the building being the responsibility of First Garden City Ltd. These facilities *"have now induced the firm to practically remove their headquarters as well as their workshops and warehouse to Letchworth from London, and they will carry on a general importing, assembling and distributing business from Letchworth as from London heretofore."*

Lloyds & Co. moved into their newly built premises in Birds Hill in 1915. As well as mowing machinery, Lloyds & Co sold a wide range of tools designed to lighten the burden of agricultural cultivation, such as the "Planet JR" range of horse and hand implements and the *Pluviette* sprinkler.

Lloyds & Co. are important to the industrial heritage of Letchworth Garden City as they represent the only remaining early Letchworth industrial pioneer. When heading towards the industrial area from the Station Road roundabout, theirs is the first low factory building on your right, at the summit of Birds Hill, which also indicates the start of the early industrial area of the town.

Their range of machinery was vast, including rotary mowers, gang mowers, hover mowers, lawn sweepers, lawn rakes, lawn sprinklers, mechanical scythes, electrical hedge trimmers, seed drills and wheel hoes, all high quality, targeting the professional specialist market. Lloyds & Co customers included college campuses, sports grounds of all kinds as well as the Crown Estates, Royal households and Chequers.

They exported equipment to all parts of the world, thanks to their great emphasis on customer care and comprehensive repair and refurbishment service. Their equipment has a worldwide reputation for quality and durability.

Advertisements for Lloyds & Co products.

The two world wars interrupted normal production, the war effort taking over. Lloyds was required to get involved in munitions manufacture. But in the post-war period it was back to the production of high-quality mowers and the company grew from strength to strength. *"We just make the best mowers in the world"*, they claimed.

Lloyds was, however, badly hit in the early part of the 1930s when the cost of importing machines was doubled and the company was threatened with closure. Mrs. E M Walker, the then Company Secretary, simply suggested that all the machines should actually be made in Letchworth and no longer imported. The company was saved and that saw the start of a boom.

It was also Mrs. Walker who, to resolve the problem of employees being laid off each autumn until the following spring, because of the seasonal nature of the work, instigated a repair service which quickly became an important part of the company's activities.

Though no longer a brand name known in every household in Letchworth, Lloyds machines have been in use not just throughout Europe but worldwide, even in places like Egypt, Argentina and Malaya, and the Paladin lawnmower presented to the Queen to mark her Silver Jubilee in 1977 is still in use at Balmoral.

Marmet Baby Carriage Syndicate Ltd

E T Morriss founded Marmet in 1912. It is an anagram of his parents' initials, E T M and A R M. In January 1913 the Marmet Baby Carriage Syndicate was registered. In October 1913 Marmet opened in the Sheds, employing thirty people and producing three to four prams a day. Business was slow to evolve in the war years as raw materials were in short supply. Once the war was over, production increased and new premises were essential. In 1920 work was started on the Nevells Building, a second wing was added in 1922 and a third in 1923. In 1919, turnover was ten times its pre-war level and the following year it doubled again.

Morriss had an innovative approach, with the aim of producing a baby carriage that would be the best of its kind: graceful, comfortable, light and reliable. His prams had a spring suspension and a tubular-steel chassis with a lifetime guarantee. The patent for this was applied for in 1920.

As far as possible all parts were made and assembled on the company premises. The company did its own tube-bending using a cold process. Wheels based on bicycle wheels were made on site. The enamelling was also on site. The bodies were made of plywood and painted in the spray shop. A sewing works produced the hoods and cushions. Marmet was the first company to standardise nickel-plated fittings, detachable and reversible folding bodies, ball-bearing quick-release wheels and cable brakes.

Marmet's achievements were recognised by:

- 1913 – certificate from the Institute of Hygiene

- 1914 – gold medallist at the Children's Welfare Exhibition

- 1917 – award from the Home Life Exhibition

- 1920 – Marmet became a member of the National Union of Manufacturers. At this time they provided their staff with a canteen and sports facilities, including tennis courts

- 1922 – exhibited at the British Industries Fair with the "world's lightest baby carriage", Marmet toy carriage and "Evasco" folding chair

- 1925 – certificate with a gold medal from the British Empire Exhibition at Wembley.

Marmet factory.

Interior of Marmet works.

In 1912 the original designs that E T Morriss had submitted to the baby trade were rejected. His response was *"Nothing becomes an earnest man better than discouragement."*

Marmet advertised actively in newspapers and orders for catalogues rapidly followed. Marmet products were in demand not only from the home market but all over the world, necessitating showrooms in North America. Patents were taken out worldwide but home demand was so great that these could not be followed up for years. In 1924 the company became Marmet Ltd with a capital of £100,000.

Marmet advertisements.

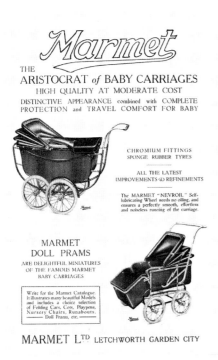

TEXTILES AND CLOTHING

St Edmundsbury Weaving Works plaques, designed by John Phillips Steele (active 1865–1948) – these were located in the entrance to the weaving works. Photographs reproduced with kind permission of the Warner Textile Archive, Braintree, Essex.

Two enterprises which arrived early in Letchworth – St Edmundsbury Weavers and the Garden City Embroidery Company – came for different, though complementary, personal and business reasons.

St Edmundsbury Weavers

St Edmundsbury Weavers was founded by Edmund Hunter (1866–1937) in 1902 in Haslemere, Surrey, then a flourishing artistic community, and came to Letchworth in 1908. He named the company after his birthplace. He and his wife Dorothea (1868–1958) visited the 1905 Cheap Cottages Exhibition *"to explore the possibility of building a small silk weaving factory"*. As theosophists and benevolent employers, they were enthused by the ethos of the emerging town and the practicalities of expanding their business in purpose-built premises with an electricity supply for power looms. Much of their staple work was for Burberry

and power looms could do this more efficiently. Further attractions offered by First Garden City Ltd were low ground rents for factory sites, reasonable commercial rates and the possibility of good housing conditions for Hunter's skilled Spitalfields weavers. The factory (originally some 12,000 square feet), at the corner of Ridge Road and Pixmore Avenue, was designed by the Letchworth architect Barry Parker (1867–1947) to look like a domestic building and, indeed, resembles Hunter's own home in Sollershott West. It was extended in 1914 and still stands. Fifty years later Dorothea wrote of Letchworth as a *"City of Dreams"* where *"home and work had one centre"* and residents' *"enthusiasm was reflected in the very active life…"*.

The Hunter family and staff in front of St Edmundsbury Weaving Works (Edmund Hunter far left, Dorothea Hunter to his left, Alec Hunter far right, all standing).

Edmund was a kind employer who allowed his staff two weeks' paid holiday a year, plus bank holidays, which was uncommon in the early twentieth century. His four skilled male weavers were paid between 39s and 47s 6d a week and the five apprentices received 5 to 15s depending on experience; eventually there were seventeen employees. In the mainstream British textile industries in 1904 a male worker's average wage was 28s 11d a week and a woman's 15s 5d. Dorothea (whose capital had funded the original business) worked in the enterprise but would not allow other married women to be employed. The couple and their two sons involved themselves in Letchworth life as active theosophists, in amateur dramatics and in folk dancing. The younger son, Alec Hunter (1899–1958) joined the firm and later made a career with

Sample of silk embroidery produced by St Edmundsbury Weaving Works, showing a typical design.

Warner & Sons, textile producers in Braintree, Essex. He claimed that Edmund preferred to design items and then see if he could sell them, an approach to doing business which eventually proved flawed.

St Edmundsbury Weavers had begun as makers on hand looms of fine ecclesiastical items like vestments, altar frontals and church hangings. They were commissioned to provide items for St Paul's Cathedral and Buckingham Palace for instance, and exhibited and won prizes at international exhibitions. Metallic thread was sometimes incorporated into the fabrics designed by Edmund, which often featured plants, animals, heraldic devices or theosophical symbols. As business flourished he realised that in order to be commercially viable he must expand production by using power looms. After the move to Letchworth he introduced some cheaper materials and produced more secular items, like dress fabric and silk scarves for Liberty. Coat linings for Burberry became the factory's main work during the First World War. A letter of May 1915 from Edmund states that he was sending to London 1 cwt of goods each week. It has been suggested that Edmund may have designed the famous Burberry "Prorsum" label. He certainly conceived and made (possibly in his own home where he added both a studio and a loom) the well-known Letchworth banner "Four Square Our City", which was carried in the 1909 May festival procession. Examples of the work of St Edmundsbury Weavers are held by Letchworth's Garden City Collection, the Victoria and Albert Museum and in St Paul's Church, Letchworth.

In the 1920s it became more difficult to sell expensively produced silk weavings as the cost of real silk soared and Edmund was obliged to use some artificial silk fabrics. In addition, Burberry began to use its own weaving works in Hampshire and major orders halved. The business was incorporated into Morton Sundour in 1928, with production at Letchworth ending in November 1931.

"A Countryman's Day Book" by C.N French, published by J. M. Dent of Letchworth in 1929.

"Forest", a woven textile designed in Letchworth, c.1910; a typical example of St Edmundsbury work.

Garden City Embroidery
(later Herz and Falk Embroidery Company)

Another significant textile enterprise which came early to the town was the Garden City Embroidery Works, later the Herz and Falk Embroidery Company, which had premises in Works Road (next to that of the Lacre Motor Company but no longer standing). Swiss embroidery and lace work are world-renowned and the firm had been founded in 1885 in St Gall, Switzerland by Max (born Marx) Herz (1860–1948). By 1891 it had an office and warehouse in London and Herz became a friend of Ebenezer Howard who encouraged him to come to Letchworth and build a factory. Indeed, Max Herz showed his commitment by buying shares in First Garden City Ltd.

The factory opened in 1907 with machinery and staff brought from Switzerland, although gradually local people replaced Swiss workers. These were mainly unmarried women who were paid 10s for a 52½ hour working week. They were provided with a sports club and a mess room for eating during their breaks. The general manager was eighteen-year-old Lewis Falk (1890 – 1954), a nephew of Herz and also from St Gall. Many years later he described Letchworth as *"a Utopia of clean, pure, air, flowers and perpetual sunshine"* in contrast to the polluted atmosphere of London and other cities. However, he recalled that to begin with it was not easy to find staff. *"There were no young people who wanted to come to work from the surrounding villages: for the girls had the traditional career of domestic service in a comfortable home and the lure of London; the boys naturally looked to the fields and quiet countryside for their future and security"…"At one stage I bought twenty bicycles [which would have cost £6–8 each] as 'inducement' for them to come to work…"*. He observed *"…how easy it is for factories in the industrial North to get workers…as against us here, sitting in an industrial oasis upon an agricultural countryside."* This was also the experience of other early manufacturers until, of course, the First World War reduced the supply of male workers and opened up opportunities to women.

During the First World War Falk served with the Middlesex Regiment as a dispatch rider and the company became a *"controlled establishment"* under the Munitions of War Act of 1915. This meant that businesses supplying the armed forces were controlled by the Ministry of Munitions, regulating wages, hours and employment conditions. All the male employees volunteered for active service (with five being killed) so work carried on with 100 women and girls making embroidered cloth badges for the British and American forces.

Over the years the company had several changes of name and by 1933 had additional premises, Lorraine Works, in Birds Hill. It closed in 1962 when demand for its products fell.

The exterior of the Garden City Embroidery factory, Works Road, c.1915.

The Spirella Company (of Great Britain) Ltd

Spirella in the early days of Letchworth Garden City

In 1909, when the five-year-old American Spirella Corset Company was looking for a site in Britain to expand its enterprise, its sympathy with the garden city's housing ideals led to the selection of Letchworth. One of Spirella's principles was that employees should work under the most attractive, healthful and sanitary conditions. Welfare was not seen as charity or paternalism but opportunity. In June 1912, Jesse Homan Pardee (one of the three original founders of Spirella) claimed that *"it is not too much to say that Spirella has accomplished something in the successful development of the first Garden City"*. Another of Spirella's founders, William Wallace Kincaid, was an idealist and Ruskinite, believing that employees should be happy, contented and *"surrounded as far as possible by the beautiful things of life"* in order to do good work. Ebenezer Howard himself linked the *"beautifying of the home life of the people with the ideal for which Spirella is working"* i.e., the beautifying of the business and working lives of the people. The company enjoyed showing visitors its amply lit and ventilated factory which was stopped for fifteen minutes every morning for the *"rest and refreshment of the employees"*. Visitors to the First Garden City often began with Spirella, the model factory.

Model advertising Spirella corset, c.1910.

Spirella was a company which sought to imbue a sense of duty and delight in work within its employees. The Spirella Creed laid out values of the responsibility of individuals, democracy, integrity, progress, mutual good-will and the importance of recreation. Even while based in the Sheds, concerts, dances, dramatic productions, folk dances, hockey and football clubs were all part of life at Spirella. Spirella, unusually for the time, employed mostly women in its factory and offices. From the very beginning, women participated fully in the various sports and other recreational activities provided by the company. The monthly journals (begun in January 1912) were primarily intended to teach and inspire its workers in the field, i.e., the corsetieres around Britain who visited women in their homes, but included news about the wider Spirella "family". The motivational language of the journals was often militaristic, likening the corsetieres to troops on the firing line and their work, study and play to warfare. The first corsetiere to be employed by the Spirella Company of Great Britain Ltd was Frances Wright of Hitchin.

Training Schools

In October 1911 Britain's First Spirella Training School was held in London. Training Schools for corsetieres all over the country quickly followed, including one in Letchworth Garden City in December of that year. By the summer of 1912 this had developed into a week-long programme. As the company was still operating from the Sheds, both the Pixmore Institute and Howard Hall were used for these early training schools, which combined recreational activities with lectures. Spirella extolled the benefits of the garden city as being a pleasant place in which to spend part of the summer break when advertising its training schools. In 1913 the first Normal Training School was held over five days in Letchworth at the end of July, followed by the National Training School in August.

Corset making in the Sheds, Spirella's early factory.

Building

Spirella worked in the Sheds while what proved to be only the initial stage of the magnificent building by the architect Cecil Hignett was planned and built (by H Hurst, builders based then at Pixmore Avenue). Space for the employment of between 500 and 600 workers, a dining room accommodating over 250 at one time, a library, rest room, reading room, roof garden promenade and recreation ground were all part of the original building begun in 1912. However, even as the fourth floor was being erected in early 1913, it was clear that the space was insufficient, and an extension was planned. By August 1913 the factory and office were installed in the new building, which included the huge assembly hall and roof garden. The roof garden was not only used for promenad concerts but by the employees on a daily basis during their rest intervals. By April 1914 the second wing was nearing completion.

Spirella in Letchworth Garden City, 1914–1920

Spirella's response to the war

Both the company and its employees initiated various activities to help those deeply affected by the war. One of the floors in the new factory was temporarily devoted to providing headquarters for the Belgian refugees newly arrived in Letchworth. Within days of the outbreak of war the workers themselves signed a petition asking for facilities to be given them for instruction in first aid and nursing. A needlework guild was formed to make garments for troops and Belgian refugees.

By December 1914 twelve Spirella employees had enlisted, which was the majority of the single male workforce. This number had risen to 24 by July 1915. The company adopted its *"usual liberal policy"* in the matter of pay and gave each recruit a definite assurance that his position would be open to him on his return. The employees remaining in Letchworth set up the Fighting Colleagues Fund and sent monthly parcels of food and cigarettes. In February 1918 50 former employees of Spirella had enlisted, which was more than 70 per cent of the entire male workforce. Many female employees had gone into National Service, munitions, government offices or were serving in France in organisations such as the WAAC.

By July 1915 Spirella employees had undertaken to maintain a bed at Letchworth Cottage

Hospital by weekly subscription. In December 1915 Spirella launched its own appeal on behalf of the War Seal Foundation (now Stoll) founded to establish homes for disabled war heroes. Spirella's intention was to raise sufficient money to fund one of these homes entirely and dedicate it *"To the memory of the relatives and friends of the British Spirella Organisation fallen on the field of honour"*. Spirella employees responded enthusiastically and just one month later, in January 1916, the Spirella employees had raised £200, half of the anticipated cost of one home, the full amount being reached just a few months later. When it was discovered that building costs had escalated because of the war, the company launched a prize offer to encourage its employees to buy more War Seals and ensure that the balance of £280 could be paid. Spirella funded scholarships for local schools, enabling local children to stay at school one year longer (until they were fifteen). By 1916, the number of these scholarships had risen to eight. The Spirella Staff Training Club included handwriting, arithmetic, office routine, English, book keeping, shorthand and typewriting classes. The Spirella Assembly Hall was lent for concerts and entertainments in aid of War Funds. In April 1918 employees began a weekly contribution to St Dunstan's Hostel for Blinded Soldiers and Sailors. By November 1920 this had amounted to £222 8s.

Poster advertising The "Great Meeting" hosted by Spirella on 29 November 1916.

Business

Like many companies, Spirella's initial response to the First World War included self-interested patriotism. It exhorted its employees to work harder and its customers to stay loyal, asserting its *"responsibility to keep the Spirella Branch of the industrial army at Letchworth…steadily employed and free from want"*. By December 1914, the company had offered an Active Service Belt to each of the 300 men from Letchworth who had joined the armed services. By February 1915 Spirella was experiencing difficulty in obtaining supplies of some materials as continental factories lay in ruins, and changed patterns and fabrics accordingly. Delays in the delivery of letters and parcels due to preference being given to the army on the railway were also causing problems. However, business expanded throughout the war, and by April 1915 the factory was working overtime through the night and had taken on 200 more workers. By December 1915 more than 30,000 Army bandoliers were made weekly in a special department. Prices for materials and wages had increased rapidly during the war but the company had absorbed the additional costs. In 1917 and again in 1918 it reluctantly increased the prices of its products. While the manufacture of ladies' corsets remained the primary function of Spirella throughout the war, in May 1918 the *Spirella Monthly* announced that:

> *Among the various contracts we handled might be mentioned those for enormous quantities of men's shirts, bandoliers and various other accessories to the accoutrement of the fighting men. At the present time we are manufacturing thousands of articles of protective clothing for the fighting forces every week. In addition to this we recently had the honour of carrying out experiments in connection with the manufacture of a special article of vast importance to a certain war Department.*

No further information or explanation is given.

Aftermath of war

On hearing of the Armistice, Spirella closed its factory and offices for the remainder of the day after the most urgent work had been finished. The Spirella Hall was used for a Thanksgiving Service on the following Sunday.

Business continued to grow as Spirella battled the world-wide shortage of materials and its own lack of space. The Assembly Hall had to be used temporarily as an office in 1919, but building was soon underway again. The company gave an undertaking that it would *"take all possible steps to find suitable employment for disabled ex-servicemen"*. The company leased ground in Willian Way for a Country Club and Recreation Ground for its employees as *"a War Memorial and thank offering to their employees for a safe emergence from the trying days of the late war"* and initiated fundraising for a new hospital in Letchworth.

In August 1920 the factory closed entirely for two weeks in order that it could be thoroughly cleaned and improvements made while the employees were on holiday. In October 1920 the last extension to the Spirella Company of Great Britain Ltd was finally completed; it was a duplicate of the very first section of the building.

The Company continued to be successful and remained in Letchworth until it finally closed in 1989. Its iconic building still stands proudly today, a testament to the town's industrial heritage.

Spirella Factory ,1918.

PRECISION MANUFACTURE

Workers at the Foster Instrument factory.

The purpose-built premises of the Foster Instrument Co., Pixmore Avenue, c.1908.
Image taken by Arthur Clutterbuck and reproduced with kind permission of Kim Fisher.

Foster Instrument Company: engineering innovation

Foster Instrument Company Ltd was founded by Charles Foster, formerly a chief draughtsman at Cambridge Scientific Instrument Co (CSI).

CSI was an early university tech spin-off: its origins lie in the workshop of a Cambridge University department established in 1878 to supply instruments for the (then) new science tripos. From there Robert Fulcher left to set up his own scientific instrument-making business, taking advantage of the increasing demand from the university for apparatus. His business was bought in 1881 by Horace Darwin – Charles's youngest son – and his friend Albert George Dew-Smith. It was renamed Cambridge Instrument Co in 1924.

Charles Edwin Foster, date unknown.

The company became a nursery for the founders of many well-known companies. William T Pye, who joined as foreman in 1880, left in 1898 to form the W G Pye Instrument Company with his son, ultimately to branch out into Pye Radio. Another member of staff, E I Everett, joined a Mr. Edgecombe to form Everett Edgecombe Ltd. S W J Stubbens, another foreman, formed Unicam Instruments Ltd. And there were others.

Foster's company came to Letchworth around 1907, possibly occupying the building which is now the café on the corner of Birds Hill and Pixmore Avenue. Charles Foster considered that garden city conditions, with the closeness of factory and home, contributed to increased productivity. He paid London wages. The company later moved into a new factory further along Pixmore Avenue.

Fosters made pyrometers (a kind of thermometer for high temperature readings, such as in furnaces) of their own design and other measuring instruments. Later they made borescopes (also known as introscopes) which allow the inspection of the inside of pipes, for example in boilers and gun barrels.

During the period 1920–1922 Charles Foster invented a new car transmission, and with A E Bowyer-Lowe (who had been chief designer at Phoenix Motors), produced a few prototype cars, known as the *Autogear*. This had a friction drive controlled automatically (by a centrifugal governor), at least for the upward changes. It gained a bronze medal in the 1922 London–Edinburgh run.

Foster Instruments eventually merged with Cambridge Instrument Co in 1971, which was then owned by George Kent Group of Luton (at the time the largest UK instrument maker), to form Foster Cambridge. The latter was taken over in 1974 by the Swiss firm of Brown Boveri (BB), and moved to St Neots. A 1988 merger between BB and the Swedish organisation ASEA resulted in the formation of ABB (ASEA Brown Boveri).

Kryptok premises, Pixmore Avenue.

In 1974 the borescope/introscope business of Foster Cambridge had been bought out by a new company, Introvision. This company continues to prosper to the present day on Avenue One in Letchworth.

Kryptok Ltd

One of the early arrivals in the first Garden City, in 1908, was an optical lens maker, Kryptok Ltd, who set up their small factory in Pixmore Avenue, close to the junction with Works Road, where the café still stands, and opposite the large building, also still standing, which was at that time the works of the printers and publishers W. H. Smith & Son Ltd.

Legend has it that Benjamin Franklin, one of the Founding Fathers of the United States, invented the bifocal lens for his eyeglasses by having the lenses of two different spectacles cut in half and wired into a single frame. Eventually this fairly crude technology was improved upon; John Louis Borsch Jr. (1873–1929) was an ophthalmologist from Philadelphia who was probably best known as the inventor of the first fused bifocal lens, which was marketed very successfully as the Kryptok lens. They were "invisible bifocal lenses", the transition between reading and distance vision lenses being much less pronounced than in earlier versions.

When Kryptok Ltd came to Letchworth in 1908 it sold (possibly under licence from the parent company) Kryptok lenses. The Letchworth company may have been established specifically to market this product in England.

Not much is documented about the early development of the factory in Letchworth, but there is evidence of their need for workers.

In C B Purdom's book *The Building of Satellite Towns*, various earlier industrial arrivals were asked: *"Has your experience of Letchworth as an industrial centre been satisfactory?"*

Kryptok Ltd's reply was *"Not altogether. Skilled lens workers prefer the amenities of a large town and country folk are difficult to train."*

In the *Biggleswade Chronicle* of 17 March 1916 it was reported that *"At the Hitchin Military Service Tribunal on Friday, Kryptok Ltd., lens makers, Letchworth, appealed for exemption for Frank Mason Mallet (19), of Arlesey, on the ground that he was indispensable."*

In November 1918 Kryptok Letchworth were advertising in newspapers as far afield as Glasgow for *"Optical Lens Workers, block and prescription, required immediately; excellent wages and permanent work; fare paid."*

In September 1919, they also advertised in the *Luton News* and *Bedfordshire Chronicle* *"WANTED immediately, general ENGINEER; all-round man; turn his hand to anything; optical machinery; good wages."*

An early 20th century advertisement for Kryptok glasses.

CO-OPERATIVE SOCIETIES AND ASSOCIATED INDUSTRIES IN LETCHWORTH

William Westall and the Garden City Co-operator horse and cart.

The co-operative movement was supportive of the experiment at Letchworth and the garden city ideal. Ebenezer Howard was keen to see co-operatives much more directly involved in the founding of Letchworth. At many conferences and events he encouraged members to invest in the venture, including setting up workshops and factories and building houses. Other Directors behind the Letchworth venture were also involved in the co-operative movement. Aneurin Williams was joint chair of the Labour Co-Partnership Association and the Executive of the Co-operative International Alliance.

Letchworth did attract a number of co-operative enterprises although these tended to be home-grown businesses and organisations. Some were more successful than others, particularly those engaged in retail or social and civic ventures. The co-operative model for industry did not fare quite so well and those involved with housing struggled and eventually disappeared.

Garden City Co-operators Ltd

Bert Williams, manager of the Garden City Press, formed the Garden City Co-operative Society in 1905, with 95 members and a share capital of £50 16s 11d. It began trading in the former Post Office at the junction of Spring Road and Baldock Road, on the edge of the garden city estate and in 1907 moved to premises in Leys Avenue built by Garden City Tenants Ltd. There were subsequent moves to other locations and the shop eventually became part of the mainstream co-operative retail movement.

A Garden City Co-operators Wheatsheaf produced by the Society's Education Committee advertised the stores and was distributed free to every household. It was also intended to help increase membership. The Co-operatives Heritage Trust website says: *"Published between 1896 and 1964, The Wheatsheaf was a monthly publication for members of co-operative societies. It was published by the Co-operative Wholesale Society and had a central section that was national, while the outside pages were published for individual consumer co-operatives and contained local news. It contained short stories, household hints and reports of events within the co-operative movement. There were also pages specifically aimed at women and children."*

Members outside Pixmore Institute, 1908.

92

Co-operators Women's Guild, GC Co-operators Ltd

Letchworth also had its own Co-operators Women's Guild, founded in 1906, but there is limited information about it, although it was still going strong in 1965, as revealed by press reports of their 59th anniversary celebrations. These Women's Co-operative Guilds promoted the involvement of women in co-operative enterprises.

Procession of the Co-operators on Norton Way South, outside the drawing offices of Parker and Unwin.

Printing

Garden City Press Ltd (GCP)

The co-operative printing enterprise of the Garden City Press Ltd, the first industry set up in connection with the new garden city is covered in detail earlier in this book. The founders of the Press were also behind a number of other co-operative industries established during the early years of Letchworth Garden City. However, the printers did not last much beyond fifteen years as a co-partnership enterprise.

Housing

Co-partnership models were used for housing schemes in Letchworth and the following illustrates two very different approaches.

Garden City Tenants Ltd

The GCP established Garden City Tenants Ltd along the same lines as earlier tenant co-operators, including Ealing Tenants, becoming part of the growing movement at that time. The first cottages were built at Eastholm Green and construction started in April 1905 so they could exhibit some as part of the 1905 Cheap Cottages Exhibition. Josiah Wedgewood MP was on the management committee, along with Sybella Gurney and Henry Vivian MP (Chair) both leading players in the national co-partnership housing movement. Bert Williams (GCP) and Harry Odell (GCP and later Wheeler, Odell & Co printers) represented tenant interests, and other members included Hugh Seebohm, Manager of Barclays Bank, Hitchin, and H Perry of Ealing Tenants Society. The prospectus states that Garden City Tenants Ltd's objects were:

To promote the erection, co-operative ownership and administration of houses for workmen and others on the Garden City Estate, by methods similar to the Tenant Co-operators Ltd. and Ealing Tenants Ltd. …

As noted in Section One, this co-partnership society made a significant and recognised contribution to provision of housing for labourers and workers of the new garden city in the run up to the First World War, building over 320 cottages across a number of small and larger estates, including:

- Eastholm
- Westholm
- Birds Hill
- Pixmore Estate
- Glebe Road
- Common View

Like many of the other co-partnership societies, GCT had a fractious existence, suffering rent strikes and accusations of high rents; they eventually sold the entire estate of 300 cottages to the Bradford Property Trust (BPT) in June 1934. The BPT became one of the largest residential property traders in the country through buying property from other model village estates including Port Sunlight and Saltaire . Tenants at Letchworth were reportedly offered the opportunity to buy their cottages through a rent purchase scheme.

Letchworth Co-operative Houses Ltd – communal living

Ebenezer Howard was conscious of the burden of domestic labour and housekeeping upon women of all classes and he believed that this could be relieved by these women sharing tasks like laundry and cooking in communal facilities. Such an arrangement would enable women to work outside the home if they wished.

In October 1907 Howard put forward his initial ideas in an issue of *The Garden City* (the quarterly journal of the Garden City Association) and two years later became a director of Letchworth Co-operative Housing Scheme (along with, among others, C Pownall, W H Knight, a Mr. Bond and Hope Rea). In 1910 the name was changed to Letchworth Co-operative Houses Ltd. The company solicited £10,000 of capital in the form of £10 mortgage debentures offering four per cent interest and by the time the scheme opened half this had been raised. The prospectus declared that:

by means of co-operative housekeeping…an important step will be taken towards the solution of the Domestic Servant Problem. The project…will be of special value to those whose incomes are comparatively small, but who wish for comfort, beauty, and order in their surroundings, and who though requiring domestic service, wish to economise in that direction.

For the servant the benefit would be that *"The nature of her work and her hours will be clearly defined, and she will be associated in it with other girls her own age."*

"Homesgarth": an experiment in communal living

The architect Henry Clapham Lander (1869–1954) was engaged to draw up plans for a scheme of 32 flats and cottages around three sides of a quadrangle on a four-acre site. There were to be several types of dwelling: one- or two-bedroom flats, each with sitting room, bathroom and WC, a pantry with sink and small gas stove (providing the means for simple meals) and three-bedroom houses, all on 99-year leases. The communal facilities included a dining room (which later became a bar, useful to Letchworth residents in the days of restricted drinking establishments), laundry, tearoom, smoking room and reading room. Outside there was an orchard, tennis courts, allotments and a bowling green. Heating and hot water were centrally provided and meals could be eaten in the dining room or sent to residents' own houses. Naturally, rents and charges – which were fairly comprehensive – varied according to the size of a person's accommodation and ranged from about £40 to £65 a year.

The communal dining room at Homesgarth, c.1911.

This experiment in communal living, originally called Homesgarth was officially opened by Ishbel Hamilton-Gordon, Marchioness of Aberdeen, on 23 November 1911, naturally in the pouring Letchworth rain! Lady Aberdeen, wife of the seventh Earl, was an unusual woman who, despite having only a minimal formal education herself, became a social activist and reformer, particularly concerned with improving the life of servants. For instance, she founded the Onwards and Upward Association which provided servant girls with correspondence courses to enhance their education. This work is, presumably, what made her a suitable public figure to open the building, as one aspect of the kind of communal domestic arrangements at Homesgarth was to supply a solution to the perceived servant problem.

Problems

At its opening, only eight houses had been completed by local builders Openshaw & Co and only half the required capital raised, although a further wing was opened by Sir Ralph Neville on 18 May 1912.

It became apparent after some years that it was difficult to ensure that the running costs of the scheme were fairly shared amongst all tenants. Although not the intention of the enterprise, the relatively high charges, the smallness of the dwellings and the lack of provision for children meant that in practice the occupants were mainly middle-class single people.

It had been intended that profits from the scheme would be reinvested in the enterprise but by the eve of the First World War it was running at a loss. Investment ceased and the communal aspect was abandoned. First Garden City Ltd took care to distance themselves from Howard's scheme for communal housing. After the war the name was briefly changed to Sollershott Court, then in 1930 to Sollershott Hall and new accommodation was made from the communal facilities. A 1934 guide to Letchworth advertised *"service flats"* at £2 15s per person, per week.

In the 1960s, 42 modern flats were added to the plot of Sollershott Hall and there are now 72 flats in total. There has been a series of freeholders through good times and bad but currently the flats are owned and managed by their occupants, who consider themselves fortunate to live in such an attractive and interesting development.

Ebenezer himself lived in Homesgarth – first at number 26 from 1915 and later at number 1 – until he left for Welwyn Garden City at the end of 1920.

Retail

Garden City Co-operators Ltd Store

The first Co-operative store was opened at Letchworth Corner, opposite the first Post Office and earliest Estate Office. From there it moved to a house on Cross Street before purpose-built premises were opened in Leys Avenue in 1907. One of those involved in the early society and the first store, F W Rodgers – in an unpublished recollection of 1905 – wrote of too few customers initially and spoiled goods which had been buried by the store manager! Things obviously improved as the society grew and expanded its enterprises and range of goods sold. To accommodate this they moved premises again and ended up on Eastcheap with a much larger store including drapery, grocery, boot and shoe, outfitting, confectionery and hardware departments.

Garden City Co-operators Stores, Leys Avenue, at its opening, 1907.

Manufacture

Woodworkers Ltd

As part of the new and growing co-partnership movement in Letchworth, the Woodworkers Ltd came in 1908 as a co-operative machine joinery and furniture manufacturer. Its manager was a Mr. Grant and the firm produced many wood products essential to building operations under way throughout the town. They would have supplied Garden City Tenants Ltd (co-partnership house builders) and many other builders active in Letchworth at that time.

As well as general wooden fixtures and fittings, quality furnishings were also produced by the Woodworkers Ltd during their time at Letchworth. The firm had a showroom at Hampstead Garden Suburb and a lovely brochure from around 1913 (held by the Garden City Collection) gives examples of their regular wares. In it they describe the business as producing their own furniture as well as commissioned pieces and customers' own designs. One very handsome example is this oak corner cabinet designed by Barry Parker – and built by the Woodworkers at Letchworth.

Given the scale and size of the works on Pixmore Avenue (apparent from the period photographs of their site) and evidence in the quotation below, it is highly likely that many of the early cottages and other buildings erected during the lifetime of this factory and workshop would have benefited from their services. If you live in one of the earlier cottages or larger houses in the town you may well have fixtures and fittings produced by this firm, or even furniture!

The Woodworkers operated at the same site throughout the early years and appear on the 1929 town plan. But limited information is available regarding the company and whether they were able to continue operating along co-partnership lines or if they had to move onto a more commercial footing like the GC Press.

A statement in the *Letchworth Magazine*, autumn 1910, says:

> Co-Partnership Tenants Ltd "…are bringing their joinery works to Letchworth; the whole of the woodwork needed for their various building schemes all over the country will be made here. They will employ some 69 or 70 joiners."

Front and rear view of the Woodworkers Ltd's extensive works, Pixmore Avenue. Images taken by Arthur Clutterbuck and reproduced with kind permission of Kim Fisher.

Interior of Woodworkers Ltd's extensive works at Pixmore Avenue. Image taken by Arthur Clutterbuck and reproduced with kind permission of Kim Fisher.

Woodworkers Ltd advertising brochure front cover, c.1913.

Civic and social facilities – Pixmore Institute

The Pixmore Institute was built in 1908 by Garden City Tenants for their members (i.e. workmen) and those of the Woodworkers to use, although it was also a facility widely enjoyed by other townspeople. The building initially included a reading room with a lending library and a billiard room and later extensions provided additional facilities. The Institute became a centre for civic and social life in the town, hosting many political meetings, plays, concerts and other events. It is recorded as the first public meeting house of the Letchworth Wesleyans prior to the building of the Wesleyan Church which opened in 1914. Eventually it became an elementary (later infant) school, which it remains today.

Photographs of the Pixmore Institute showing the Institute as it was originally built and then after later extensions to provide additional facilities.

PHOTOGRAPHY AND CINEMA

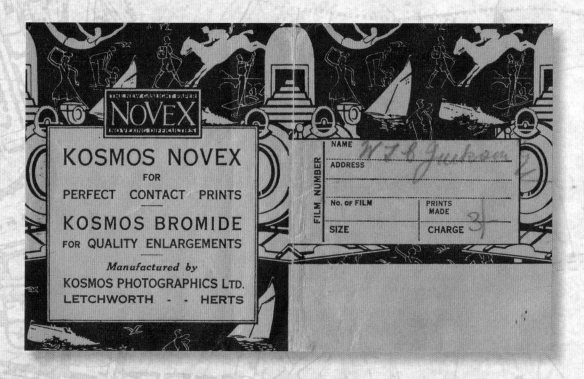

Kosmos Photographics envelope advertising their NoVex photographic paper c.1920s.

Kinora Ltd

The Kinora was an early motion-picture device, a form of "mutoscope" designed by Auguste and Louis Lumière, which appeared in England around the end of the nineteenth century and was manufactured from 1909 to 1914 in Letchworth by Kinora Ltd.

The Kinora worked like a flip book or a Rolodex, using images which were conventional monochrome photographic prints fixed to strong, flexible, cards attached to a circular core. As it was unable to project pictures it could only be used by one or two people at a time, so was most suitable for home use. In the years before the First World War the Kinora was the most popular medium for viewing home movies in the United Kingdom.

A viewer rotates the handle that is connected to a 14 cm diameter wheel. The wheel contains a set of small pictures that are each seen individually in front of a lens. If the wheel is turned at the right speed the combination of pictures give the illusion of motion. Each reel usually holds about 25 seconds of motion.

The manufacturers, Kinora Ltd, developed the invention of the Lumières. To begin with they supplied a range of moving picture reels produced from professional photographs, which could be bought or hired. There were over 600 different reels available. Later, owners of a Kinora could have their own motion films produced by a professional photographer. Later still, beginning in 1908, the company supplied a special camera, accompanied by rolls of photographic paper or celluloid one inch wide, to enable people to make their own movies. These could be sent to the company for processing.

The Kinora was the most successful home-movie machine in Britain before 1912. It is interesting to note that, seventeen years earlier, the Lumière brothers had created a device capable of projecting movies to large audiences. Many today consider their invention, the *Cinématographe*, the start of modern cinema. Yet despite the public's new-found interest in projected movies the Kinora continued to be highly popular in Britain for nearly twenty years after the birth of cinema.

Kinora viewer.

It is not known where the reels and machines were actually manufactured before 1909 but in that year a purpose-built factory, said to be capable of producing 5,000 Kinora reels a week, was opened on the east side of Pixmore Avenue, Letchworth, situated between Phoenix Motors and the Garden City Laundry, where the new estates of Phoenix Drive and Ascot Drive now stand. Within three years the workforce employed there numbered a hundred men and women. Such an intensive system of production meant that reels could be offered to the public at much cheaper prices than before.

The middle classes originally saw attendance at the cinema in its early days as socially undesirable as it had developed from fairground-like shows. Variety acts were mixed with the showing of short films. The Kinora provided that middle stratum of society with moving pictures at home so that they did not have to go to the theatre and thus could avoid mixing with the lower classes. The cost of a Kinora viewer ranged from £5 to £16, so was beyond the reach of most working-class families. Perhaps the Kinora encouraged greater social stratification. Cinema, though, essentially led to the demise of the Kinora.

As reported in The *Citizen* on 7 January 1914 the Letchworth factory was burnt out, with damage estimated at £25,000 to £30,000, covered by the insurance. By then the cinema screen held greater attractions than the Kinora and the company did not rebuild the lost factory.

Some of the aspects of the Kinora survive in modern media entertainment. Home video rental was until recently a major part of distribution in the film business and its roots were in the availability of Kinora reels for lease. Personal hand-held recording devices also saw their beginning with the Kinora. Hand-held cameras embodied in mobile phones are much used today to capture important aspects of our individual lives.

Kosmos Photographics Ltd

In January 1958 Kosmos Photographics Ltd, a nationally and internationally known company, which had occupied its site on Pixmore Avenue, Letchworth Garden City, for about 50 years, ceased production. Its 70 employees were largely absorbed by the many other industries in the area.

The company arrived in the garden city in 1908 and occupied a site on Pixmore Avenue, where it would eventually be sandwiched between the Garden City Press Ltd (arrived 1905) and Woodworkers Ltd (arrived 1910), on the west side of Pixmore Avenue, almost opposite where it joins Ridge Road.

Kosmos Photographics was concerned at the beginning with the manufacture of bromide papers only and employed fifteen to twenty workers. A new chloro-bromide paper called Vitegas was introduced, which brought rapidly increased expansion to the business. During the First World War the company supplied very large consignments of bromide to the British military flying service which became the Royal Air Force.

Not much is recorded about the company's early days in the garden city, although they do feature in a tax law case – Kosmos Photographics Ltd v CIR (1919) 1 ATC 61 – which alleged the company was bankrupt and was then bought by a newly incorporated company of the same name, and with the same shareholders as the old company, apart from its bank. The case was lost by the company.

Kosmos employees outside factory (later image from 1930s).

Most of their development into a very successful company, making a complete range of sensitised photographic papers for industrial, commercial and professional photographers, advertising specialists and postcard publishers, and employing 70, took place after our period, following the firm's big expansion in the early twenties, and will be a subject for future study.

A footnote – something of local interest but occurring beyond the period under our study: in 1924, Kosmos commissioned a new building, praised by some architects for *"dispelling the myths that concrete cannot be beautiful"*. The building was inspired by Howard Carter's explorations of Egypt, a giant art deco factory regarded as *"expressive of an art gallery or public library"*, qualified by the firm's business being *"closely allied to art"*. It was the building we now know as Tesco in Baldock.

Kosmos became insolvent before ever moving into the factory and four years later in 1928 the empty building was taken over by the Yorkshire-based Full-Fashion Hosiery Company, becoming Kayser Bondor in 1936.

Going to the pictures in the early garden city

The first public performances of films with a paying audience in Great Britain began at the Polytechnic in Upper Regent Street, central London, on 21 February 1896. Consisting of short films made in France by the Lumière brothers and shown via their *Cinématographe* equipment, the programme was so successful that it transferred to the Empire Music Hall in Leicester Square and was one of the top items on the bill.

The showing of moving pictures then spread rapidly through travelling fairs, by showmen hiring local halls for special shows, and through the music halls. Businessmen began taking over shops, halls and railway arches, painting over the windows and otherwise rather crudely converting them into full-time cinemas. A more elaborate variation involved a hall adapted to resemble a railway carriage presenting moving views (*"Tours of the World"*) that had been photographed along railway lines, pre-dating by more than a hundred years today's YouTube cab-view rides on modern trains.

With the Cinematograph Act of 1909, new regulations came into effect to improve safety. As the nitrate film stock being projected was highly flammable, the Act required the provision of a fire-resistant projection booth. This legislation greatly encouraged the spread of purpose-built picture houses. These usually had gaudy outside designs to catch the eye, with ticket booths open to the street, and the frequent use of the word "Electric" in their names as a reminder that electricity was something of a novelty. Shows were made up of short films, including travelogues and news items, and lasted only for 60 to 90 minutes (feature films began to arrive around 1914), so these early cinemas were generally provided with tiny foyers and few toilet facilities.

The Palace Cinema.

The new town of Letchworth Garden City was not behind in these developments. On Monday 6 December 1909 the Palace cinema, known as the Letchworth Picture Palace, opened in Eastcheap. It was brought to the town by film pioneer Arthur Melbourne-Cooper, following his successful opening of the Alpha in St Albans. The architects were Barry Parker and Raymond Unwin and the builders Bennett Bros. There were two shops incorporated into the frontage and seats for 750 on a sloping floor, priced at four pence or six pence, or two pence for more spartan accommodation, but also eight boxes at the back, each seating five and costing three shillings. Seats could be booked in advance, and you could store your bicycle for free. The programmes changed twice weekly.

The Palace is said to be the first building in the town centre to be provided with electricity from the new generator which had been established in Works Road in 1907.

The fire station arrived next door to the Palace in 1911.

Letchworth Picture Palace

SATURDAY, APRIL 17th

(At the 8 o'clock performance only)

Positively the LAST Presentation of the Successful Revue

'PASS ALONG PLEASE'

A Fantasy in 3 Scenes

WEDNESDAY, APRIL 21st. SPANISH NIGHT

including the successful Musical Comedietta

'SUNNY SEVILLE'

SUNDAY, TUESDAY & WEDNESDAY, JUNE 7th, 8th, & 9th

'ENMESHED BY FATE INTO THE WILDERNESS'

THURSDAY, FRIDAY, & SATURDAY, JUNE 10th, 11th & 12th

'NIGHT RIDERS OF PETERSHAM'

'HONOUR OF THE LAW'

Every evening at 8. Saturdays at 6 & 8. Matinee on Saturday at 3

A recreated advertisement from The Citizen, April 1914, advertising plays and films.

SERVICE INDUSTRIES

E H Wightman, Drapers & Dyers' Agents & Haberdashers, Hosiers & Milliners, Leys Avenue.

The Pioneer (Garden City) Laundry, Pixmore Avenue

In 1909 the Pioneer (Garden City) Laundry was established with purpose-built premises. The laundry was established by Charles Francis Townsend and a Mr. Jackson and Townsend also designed the machinery and specified the chemicals to be used. It appears that Letchworth has a link to a prominent individual associated with the development of laundries at the time. Townsend was Assistant Examiner at the Royal College of Physicians, a freelance writer and also editor of the British trade magazine *The Power Laundry*.

Whether Townsend actually designed the building is debatable as the plan shown for a proposed steam laundry (dated May 1908) suggests the architects were Howard Goadby and Marrian, Twickenham. Johnsons Apparel, who are based in the old laundry building, have crompared this plan with the site today and confirmed it could well be an early design and layout plan.

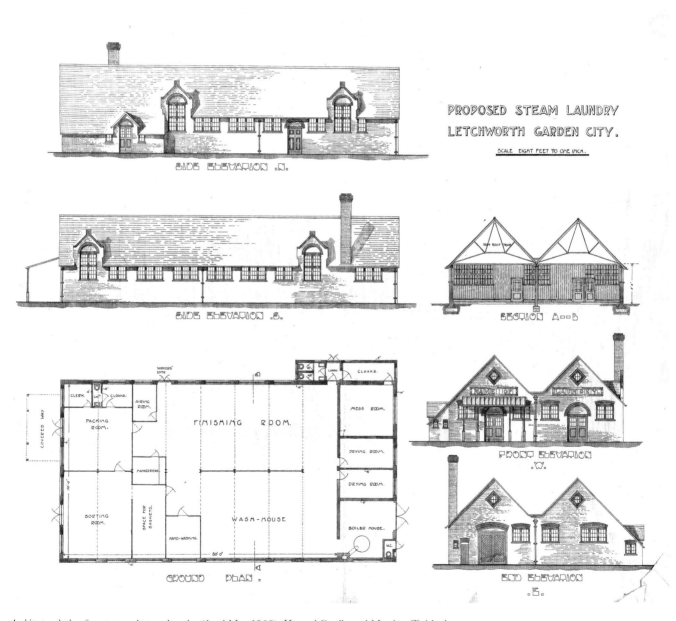

Architectural plan for a proposed steam laundry (dated May 1908), Howard Goadby and Marrian, Twickenham.

Example of a steam laundry interior, c.1907/08. Image provided by Johnson Apparel, Letchworth.

The Pioneer Laundry offered a range of services, including washing, dry cleaning, dyeing and carpet beating. Early Letchworth Directories show that the laundry was known by a number of names, including The Letchworth Garden City Laundry and Pioneer (Garden City) Laundry. It would have been a steam laundry, fitted out with the latest technology of the time, no doubt taking advantage of the availability of electric power at Letchworth.

Although no early images have been found of the interior, it is likely to have been similar to the image above.

Townsend's laundry was one of three laundries which operated in Letchworth in the early days, so there was healthy competition. The first laundry service established in the new industrial area was in 1907. This was run by Miss M Miller as The Home Laundry and located opposite the Garden City Press Ltd on Pixmore Avenue. This is likely to have been a much smaller operation than that of the Pioneer Laundry.

Pioneer Laundry Exterior.

Carpet beaters at work, Pioneer Laundry.

The development of shops in Letchworth, 1903–1914

To the regret of Ebenezer Howard, the growth of shops in the garden city did not happen as he envisaged and would have wished. In his 1902 book *Garden Cities of To-Morrow* he set out (and illustrated with diagrams) his vision for a centrally located shopping centre, *"a wide glass arcade called the 'Crystal Palace' "* which would contain covered shops and also function as a *"Winter Garden"* for recreation. He wrote of the important relationship, as he saw it, between *"municipal and individual enterprise"*; whilst a manufacturer was not wholly dependent on the custom of the town, a retailer was and would wish his competitors to be limited. Howard discussed how to attract shopkeepers to the town whilst avoiding both wasteful duplication and *"the evils attending monopoly"*. As FGC Ltd was the sole landlord of the town it was able to control (through the leases it granted) the number and type of shops permitted and reap the revenue from leases and rents. If the shops were satisfactory they would be allowed to continue; if they lost the public's goodwill, a competitor would be permitted to start up. This principle Howard termed the *"local option"*. He further hoped that such arrangements would result in good employment conditions for shop staff.

C B Purdom, chronicler of the development of Letchworth, quoted Howard's later observations: *"The shopping system of Letchworth is now very much on conventional lines, not at all what it might have been if sufficient imagination and enterprise had been brought into play..."* The promoters of Letchworth had failed to persuade any of the pre-existing co-operative societies to set up stores in the town: *"the pioneers of the co-operative movement...regarded the first garden city as a wellnigh hopeless experiment, and so took no active part in it."* In contrast, when Welwyn Garden City was being established from 1920, Second Garden City Ltd created Welwyn Stores Ltd to provide shopping facilities for the town, thereby retaining a controlling interest in retailing for the first ten years. The shops of Letchworth came about in a piecemeal manner, by private enterprise. Some were branches of existing retailers from neighbouring towns; others were set up by pioneers who saw opportunities in the garden city and embraced the challenge of running a business for an initially small population.

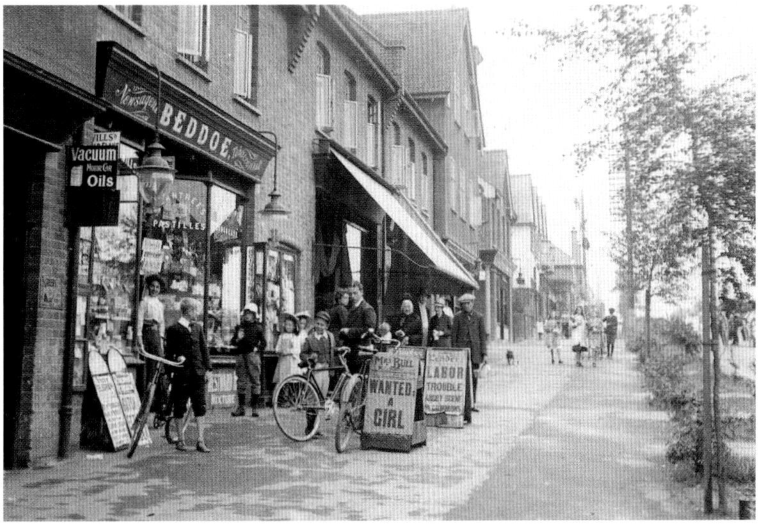
BEDDOE
Vacuum
Oils
LABOR
TROUBLE
WANTED
A
GIRL

Beddoe, newsagent and tobacconist, Station Road, c.1905.

The first sites for shops were plots in Station Road, available from June 1905 at ground rents of between £1 16s 3d and £3 2s 6d per annum for a 99-year lease. Eight of the nine plots offered were let by the following year, together with four other shop sites in Leys Avenue. The premises were small, with living accommodation above, and in a variety of architectural styles. Purdom states that half the shops were erected by the Company for letting on a lease and half built by the shopkeepers themselves. By July 1907, when the first Letchworth Directory was published, there were around 30 shops, serving most of the everyday needs of the residents.

We find, for example, three bakers, a butcher, a health-food store, three newsagents, a fishmonger, a fruiterer and four grocers. The first shop seems to have been a Garden City Stores and Post Office, run from 1905 by the postmaster Henry Cullip in Station Road. Some shops sold more than one type of product and there were also sales from private houses, farms and smallholdings, the latter through a short-lived co-operative enterprise called Garden City Small Holdings Ltd. It failed because oversupply alternated with shortage and, with a town population of 5,250 in 1908, the market was restricted.

Bennett's Business Directory for Hertfordshire of 1914 shows how the early shopkeepers sold diverse goods and services. G F Armitage and Co. were listed as selling *"plumbers goods, cycles and accessories, gas fittings, electrical goods etc."* [sic] W A Holmes at The Conservatory in Station Road was a *"seed grower and merchant"* and Fred Jarden kept a livery stable in Station Road and a fishmonger's shop in Eastcheap. Some early businesses were short-lived, like Wells' tailoring business and G Cramp's drapery (although the latter proprietor is an example of a citizen who also involved himself in civic affairs, in his case as a parish councillor), simply because there were too few customers among the pioneer population. In addition, many families could be largely self-sufficient in produce from their own gardens. During the First World War shop building ceased, although by August 1920 there were 82 shops in Letchworth.

In the earliest days of the garden city, retailers from nearby towns like Hitchin and Baldock delivered goods to the new residents. In the case of alcohol this service continued for several decades whilst Letchworth remained a "dry" town. Subsequently, some of these businesses, such as T Brooker, ironmonger and house furnisher, and W B Moss & Son, grocer, established Letchworth branches, both in Leys Avenue. An early occupant of Station Road in 1906 (having started in Hitchin in 1808) was the butcher Charles F Ansell and W. H. Smith & Son still trade at their original site in the town. It is interesting to note how some of these early retailers sold a number of unrelated goods or services or changed what they offered over time.

E and E H Housden advertised in the 1907 Directory, as City Stores and Café. Ebenezer H Housden was the first Secretary of Letchworth's Chamber of Commerce, from November 1907, and later Secretary of the Letchworth Tradesmen's Protection Society, founded in 1910; presumably, even in a place like the garden city, such a body was thought necessary to look after the interests of business people. The shop sold homeopathic and patent medicines, toilet and household requisites, photographic materials, and offered tea and cakes in the adjacent café. Their premises at 17 Station Road may be the last surviving original shop front in Letchworth designed by the Parker and Unwin practice. In the 1911 Census Emily Hare Housden (possibly Ebenezer's unmarried daughter) gave her occupation as a shopkeeper selling *"Toys, Wools and Fancy Goods"* from the same address.

An unusual shop which reflected the interest in handmade crafts and healthful living within the town was The Crockery, in business from 1908 to 1935, first in Leys Avenue and later Station Place. It sold only leadless glazed items, notably those produced by the Iceni Pottery (referred to later), started in Letchworth in about 1907. There was, in the end, some co-operative commerce in the town, as hoped for by the pioneer developers.

Most of the earliest shops were, as has been seen, independent businesses, set up with some degree of faith by people who embraced the ethos of the garden city. Nevertheless, branches of well-known national chains also came to the town. Letchworth gained a handsome Post Office building in Broadway in 1912 (in addition to the existing village post offices), and by July 1907 there were branches of Barclays and Midland banks, W. H. Smith & Son newsagents, and in the following years Boots the Chemist. By the end of 1909 two shops had opened at Norton Corner to serve those living further from the centre. The original master plan for Letchworth, drawn up by Parker and Unwin, envisaged a second shopping street to be called *Westcheap* but this was never developed. Other failed ideas are reflected in the haphazard growth of The Wynd and the lack of a successful area for an open-air market. Various locations were tried but it didn't last, probably because of competition from the charter markets in Hitchin and Baldock.

It is clear that, despite Ebenezer Howard's misgivings, Letchworth developed a thriving shopping community which provided for most residents' needs. In the main this was through private enterprise and investment in independently run shops, many of which are fondly remembered by local people. Then, as now, a useful, rather than an exciting, shopping experience!

COTTAGE INDUSTRIES

40 Gernon Road, the premises of the Busyville Knitting Industry, c.1920.

Cottage industries in early Letchworth

The developers of the new town, First Garden City Ltd, actively encouraged businesses and manufacturers to move there. They also fostered an atmosphere which attracted the kind of people who wanted to combine living in a pioneering community with carrying on a small enterprise, what we might call a cottage industry. Indeed, some literally operated from cottages or smallholdings.

Letchworth Directories of various dates record a range of activities of this type, including beekeeping, blacksmithing (presumably making window and door fittings for the new houses, as well as the usual agricultural items), boot- and shoe-making, dressmaking, an organ builder and a visiting artificial-teeth-maker. About most there is minimal information but others can help give a more rounded picture of commercial life in the early years of the town.

In the early twentieth century most women made their own clothes or had them made by a local dressmaker. In 1905, for example, Miss Martha Webb set herself up at Hope Cottage, 337 Norton Way South. (She was later a nurse at the Spirella Company.) Mrs. Tackley advertised in the July 1907 Directory as *"First Class Dressmaker"*, operating from 24 Birds Hill and in 1912 Madame Stepniak advertised her *"Russian Peasant Work / Handmade goods in Linen, Lace, Embroideries, Toys, Woodwork, Metal Work (buttons, clasps, chains etc.), obtained from Madame Stepniak, Oblomkova, Norton Road, Letchworth"*. Many residents kept beehives in their gardens, allotments or smallholdings and must have sold some of their produce. The Garden City Horticultural Society, set up in 1906, had classes for honey in its shows.

The simple premises of Iceni Pottery at the junction of Green Lane and Works Road.

Some activities grew from small beginnings to become medium-sized commercial enterprises. The Busyville Knitting Industry seems to have begun about 1908 as a collective of hand knitters at the famous Round House cottage, 140 Wilbury Road. This radical, sixteen-sided, pre-fabricated concrete building was erected for the 1905 Cheap Cottages Exhibition and the 1911 Directory lists the proprietor, Richard Haworth, as living there. (He was later the first secretary of Letchworth Rotary Club, set up in 1924.) In 1915 the business was at *Little Roof*, 1 Lytton Avenue, formerly the studio of the artist Jessie Pym, and described as a *"knitted goods manufacturer"*. There were subsequent moves to premises at 39 Leys Avenue and, by the early 1920s, seemingly purpose-built accommodation in Gernon Road. Production was no longer hand work but machine made.

A variety of small enterprises

The Directory of 1910 reveals that there was, perhaps surprisingly, an organ builder in Letchworth. Ambrose William Hayter had works at 105A Pixmore Way. By 1914 the business was A W Hayter & Son, Garden City Organ Works (the son being Lawrence Hayter, an illustrator, designer of bookplates and prominent vegetarian). While serving as a member of the sixth Bedfordshire Regiment Lawrence was killed in action in December 1917. The works seems to have carried on until at least 1937.

The garden city attracted unconventional people, including those who favoured so-called rational dress, like unstructured dresses for women and soft shirts and no hats for men. Sandals rather than shoes were believed to be better for the feet, allowing them to breathe, and there are photographs of adult and child pioneers wearing the (in)famous Letchworth sandals. These would have been made by local maker George Adams (1859–1910) at his home in Croft Lane, Norton, then quite an artists' colony. He had grown up in Sheffield with a cobbler father and through the local Socialist movement came to know the poet and campaigner Edward Carpenter who introduced him to Indian-style sandals when he joined his commune at Millthorpe, Derbyshire. Adams and his family came to Letchworth around 1905, attracted by the ethos of the town, and made sandals, including a *Millthorpe* style for about 10s 6d for an adult pair. Like other pioneer residents, Adams had more than one occupation as he was also a gardener and beekeeper and worked at the Iceni Pottery.

A renowned pottery

The Iceni company became nationally and even internationally recognised for its output of beautiful lustre-glazed earthenware whose distinguishing feature was that the glazes used did not contain the injurious lead of many commercially produced wares. The pottery was set up about 1907/8 in a collaboration between Annie Jane Lawrence (who commissioned the radical Letchworth adult school called The Cloisters) and her architect, the multi-talented William Harrison Cowlishaw. It seems to have occupied two sites, first at the junction of Works Road and Green Lane and from about 1913 east of Dunhams Lane, near the gas works, in a simple wooden building of about 800 square feet. It went by the name of Iceni (presumably after the East Anglian Iron Age tribe who travelled along the Icknield Way which passes through Letchworth) but was also called Garden City Pottery Works. Items were made in small numbers or as commissions and stamped ICENI or ICENI/LEADLESS/LETCHWORTH. Most were decorated with a monochrome glaze, a few were painted or had pierced decoration. Pieces were exhibited at prestigious exhibitions at home and abroad and sold through a shop at 3 Leys Avenue, Letchworth (The Crockery, mentioned above). The volume of production was necessarily small and today items are rare, although the Garden City Collection holds a representative sample. In 1913, a fire at the works destroyed many pottery moulds and items prepared for an international exhibition but the final blow was the outbreak of war in 1914 when the pottery

THE CITIZEN, LETCHWORTH, SEPTEMBER 24th, 1926

A LETCHWORTH INDUSTRY

Copyright]   *[A. Clutterbuck*

Organ built by A W Hayter, later Garden City Organ Builders, Pixmore Way.

Charcoal drawing dated 1899 of sandal maker and potter George Adams by his friend the artist C J Fox.

closed. The building was used for other purposes but there is now no trace of this short-lived craft enterprise which so epitomised the Arts and Crafts leanings of early Letchworth.

The creative atmosphere of the Garden City naturally attracted as residents many architects and artists, some of national renown. They were able to maintain connections with London whilst finding inspiration in the nearby countryside. Important artists like Harold Gilman, Spencer Gore and William Ratcliffe depicted the growing town. Lesser known, in some cases, semi-amateur artists who lived here (mainly in the Croft Lane and Sollershott areas) include Sarah Birch, Juliet Branson, Edward Docker, Charles James Fox, Frank Stanley Ogilvie and Onslow Whiting.

The Census of 1911 was, of course, the first to include the new garden city and analysis of it reveals the numbers of people who declared their occupation from a range of categories prescribed by the census authority. For instance, eleven residents described themselves as artists of various kinds; of these, some were well-known, others probably simply amateurs. Another ten people were craft workers of other kinds, such as upholsterers, embroiderers, a watch and jewellery maker, a frame maker and a sign writer. There were 21 dressmakers or tailors, three milliners, six bootmakers or repairers, three hairdressers and seven blacksmiths/farriers. In addition, individual "self-employed" workers included a cabinet maker, coppersmith, tinsmith, paper hanger, window cleaner, piano tuner and a herbalist. It is obvious that these workers (some of whom might have had more than one occupation) were providing necessary services for their fellow residents, a demonstration of the self-sufficiency of early Letchworth.

Three small earthenware bowls with lustre glazes, c.1907-1914, from the collection of North Hertfordshire Museum. Image reproduced with kind permission of North Hertfordshire Museum.

TENEMENT FACTORY: MULTI-INDUSTRY FACILITIES

Front view, First Garden City Tenement Factory, Works Road. This building is still standing (albeit currently disused) and is now called Vantage Point.

First Garden City Ltd Tenement Factory, Works Road

The *Hive*, or Tenement Factory, built by FGC Ltd was finished in 1914 and designed for sub-division into a number of complete factories. It provided three floors of space, each around 5,000 square feet, and was intended for smaller manufacturers, much like incubation space today. One of its features, which FGC Ltd promoted, was that it was relatively fireproof through the small division of space; factory fires were a real concern for manufacturers at the time. Tally-Ho Motor Company from Australia, Remus Machinery Company and Messrs. Thomson and Kindred, jam makers, were the first tenants in 1914. Remus were manufacturers of cardboard box-making machinery, previously made in Germany. The Tenement Factory was a real success and the Company reported that it was soon fully let and such was the demand that they could do with building another.

Contemporary advertisement for Thomson and Kindred, Letchworth.

Crayola and Letchworth

In 1915 Binney & Smith, the American company behind the globally renowned Crayola brand, leased a section of the new Tenement Factory. An article in the Garden City Association journal from July 1915 said that the Binney & Smith Company opened a UK branch of their very large New York works, making chalk and crayon pencils using chalk from local chalk pits. Before this chalk crayons were not made in the UK but imported from America. The chalk was almost certainly extracted from north Hertfordshire chalk, pits including at Norton.

Binney & Smith (Europe) Ltd, Bedford, have confirmed that the company set up in Letchworth. The UK enterprise became known as the Cosmic Crayon Company and was a joint venture by Binney & Smith with American Crayon. It was incorporated on 9 May 1916. The company moved from Letchworth to Bedford in late 1918, as they sought larger premises. Binney & Smith (Europe) Ltd are still based in Bedford but

Rear view, First Garden City Tenement Factory, showing loading bays.

its manufacturing operations transferred back to America in late 2003. One of the final packets of Crayola crayons produced in the UK was displayed during Letchworth Local History Group's 2015 Exhibition on the early industries, along with a 75th Anniversary presentation crayon and a 2003 Centenary presentation box only available for company employees and retirees. These were kindly loaned by Binney & Smith (Europe) Ltd. Letchworth played an important part in the establishment of Crayola in the UK.

HOW THE WAR AFFECTED LETCHWORTH

LETCHWORTH'S ROLL OF HONOUR

LONG LIST OF GARDEN CITY MEN WHO ARE SERVING THEIR COUNTRY

"HONOUR THE BRAVE"

Citizens of Letchworth will glance with pride over the long list of local men who are serving their country in the Army or Navy.

During the past few weeks we have noted in our columns the departure of one and the other to join His Majesty's forces. This week we have endeavoured to make the list on Letchworth's Roll of Honour fuller and more complete. We have found it a difficult but pleasing task. There is of course, no official list to draw from, and we have frequently had merely a casual conversation as our only source of information regarding some name in the list. In some cases the regiments are given, generally where a regiment is not stated the men have joined Lord Kitchener's Army. Several of the names are repeated but

we have given thought that even where the names are also given under another heading such as "Territorials" it is very desirable that the men enlisting or called up from any particular factory should be grouped together, from considerations of esprit de corps, if nothing else.

We shall be sorry if any names have been omitted, because we had no information regarding them, and we shall be very pleased to publish a supplementary list of any further names sent to the "Citizen" Office.

The list will, however, serve to indicate how splendid has been the response to the call to arms in the Garden City and its immediate surroundings. It will also help us to realise the debt of gratitude we owe to the many

brave young fellows and middle-aged men, too many of them married, who have given up good positions, comfortable houses, and their beloved association with "their ain folks", for the rough, and often comfortless and dangerous, life of a soldier in this great national crisis.

All honour and praise to our brave fellows from Letchworth! They are not forgotten and their sacrifice for their country will be fondly remembered by every citizen.

The following is a list of employees of the various local firms who have been called to the colours, or who have enlisted in His Majesty's Army.

FIRST GARDEN CITY LIMITED
Ernest Plum
Ernest Wood
Oscar Eaton (Herts Yeomanry)
Charles James (Reservist RGA)
Henry Mabbitt
(Herts Territorials)
William Gilbert (Reservist)
William Ashwell
Herbert Cooper
E Lovegrove (Herts Territorials)
George Pike
(Army Service Corps)
Joseph Hubbard
James Seymour (RAMC)
H Anger
George Clark (7th Royal Fusiliers)

GARDEN CITY PRESS
C Lake
R Sullivan
J Satterthwaite
F Darley
A W Fox
R W Hazard
J Newman
L Parkes
H A Loughman
J Bowskill
J Plume

MESSRS. EWART & SONS LTD
J Ashwell
T Futter
E J Gray
H Cox
C Turner
W Smith
H Nickerson
F Gray
G Sherwood
C Dean
R Redding
R Macdonald
E Gray
B Phillips
B Day
G Hyde
H B Dowcra
E Monk
F Wilkinson
T Munt
H Smith
L Smith
S Bishop
J Witherden
L Upchurch
H Taylor
F Brazier
J O'Brien
A Hughes
S Gentle
C Andrews

B V Gray
B Vine
H Christopher
E Parker
A Monk
A King
A Clarke
K Kitchener
H Cook
E Strudwick
C Chalkley
J French
A Trowbridge
A Swain
V Flanders
H Tasker
C Kitchener
S Ashton
B Watts

PHOENIX MOTOR WORKS
F Ashwell
Geo Ashton
Geo Wyatt
L V Lines
L A M Randover
T Bogaersto (Belgium)
H H Davis
T Williamson
W Cook
N Brown
H E Brothers
J Fairclough (Navy)
W Flanders
C Brandon
D Brown
H Hansen

LACRE MOTOR WORKS
Sergt H Tristram (Royal Marines)
A Burnett (Royal Navy)
W E Carter
(Royal Horse Guards)
A R Bickerstaff (Royal Navy)
H Finney (Royal Engineers)
E Garner (Royal Engineers)
W Anthony (Royal Navy)
G Glover
C Freeman (Imp Yeomanry)
F E Sherras (Territorials)
B Mustins (Royal Navy)
A Wadsworth (Royal Engineers)
Col Sergt Dawson
F Drewitt
W L Hopkins

The following have been told to hold themselves in readiness

W Ringer (Royal Navy)
E H Sanders (Royal Navy)
R L Summindenger (Royal Navy)
W E Clifton (Royal Navy)

The following ex Lacre men are also serving their country

J Moore (ASC)
E F Lee (Royal Navy)
W E Mattingley (Royal Navy)
W R Mullinger (Royal Navy)
B A Bagnall (Royal Engineers)
L Pettengell
(Army Service Corps)
A Pettengell
(Army Service Corps)
R Downey (Army Ordnance)
K Inwards
(Royal Engineers)

WOODWORKERS LIMITED
F Welsh
H Levitt
H Cotton
H Haddrell
A L Smith

The above have joined the Territorials

A E Collins
E W Pilsworth
A Osborn
S G Kingsley
H Bates
W Vivian
E J Garrett

J M DENT & SON LTD
E Woodlove
A Wilkinson
W Barber
J Hawkins
W Mahew
H Whitley
F Pollard
H Ware
C Walle
C Webb
Owen Brown
Stanley Walker (Territorials)
Chas Levitt (Territorials)
Douglas Chisholme (Territorials)
Ben Bates
Jack Busby
E Gray
T Brandon
W Copham
W Coleman
T Northwood
E Ryder
F Burgess
T Connolley (Naval Reserve)
B Hyde
H Hawkes

ARDEN PRESS
T Woodroff (RAMC)
H Cartland (RAMC)
W Lees
S Downs (Kent Regt)
W Evans (Kent Regt)

W Faggetter (Middlesex)
L Millbank (Bedfordshire)
J Portens (Bedfordshire)
E Perkins (Bedfordshire)
F Brimscombe (Bedfordshire)
E Cripps (Horse Guards Blue)

COUNTRY GENTLEMEN'S ASSOCIATION
F W Broomhall
H Davy

HEATLY GRESHAM ENGINEERING COMPANY
C Maylin
A Huckle
F Nicholls
S Sheppard
A Robinson
H Denton
L Ellis
H Peters
S Rowe
J Davies
F Cooper
F Dear
G Tindall
E Gray
A T Smith
L Wright
S Cooper
W Wilkins
G Adcock
W Sutton
W Sampson
W Warman
R Monk
J Corkett
E Coleman
H Smith
P Hunt
J Jordan
G Field

SPIRELLA
L Pettengell
F Hook
A H Armshaw (Kitchener's Army)
A Isenchmid (Swiss Army)
E Curry (Beds Yeomanry)
A E Boardman (Herts Territorials)
H V Foster (Beds Yeomanry)
E Berrett (Kitchener's Army)

The Spirella Company have also organised a Rifle Club, and an Ambulance and First Aid Corps, the latter having fifty members.

W B MOSS & SON
J Purfield
O F Lake
H S Smith
H Minnis
F Wilmott

Extract from Letchworth's "Roll of Honour", published in The Citizen, 18 September 1914, listing industries and their men who joined up.

How the First World War affected the town

In August 1914, when war broke out, Letchworth Garden City was just nine years old and recognised as a success, having established a diverse and significant industrial base and a population that continued to grow. By 1914 the town's population was 8,500, rising to 9,000 by January 1915. It was also regarded as a healthy place to live with a death rate per thousand (in 1913) almost half that recorded nationally.

Reports in *The Citizen* for 1914 suggest an expectation that the war would be over swiftly, which was, of course, not the case. The garden city was still evolving and in terms of the grand plan certainly not finished. First Garden City Ltd took the decision to continue with its plans insofar as was reasonably possible throughout the war. However, whilst Letchworth continued to thrive as a place where people wanted to live and the industrial base grew, finishing the development of the garden city was hampered by restrictions on building and increased costs during the war years. It was not until the middle of 1919 that Company records suggest things were returning to normal and development was picking up again.

Wartime advertisement for E H Wightman drapery, Leys Avenue, published in The Citizen newspaper, October 1914.

Even during the war Letchworth managed to attract new industries, including Kryn & Lahy with a purpose-built munitions factory recruiting the thousands of Belgian refugees in England. By 1915 the population was estimated to be approaching 12,000, with nearly 3,000 said to be Belgians. Letchworth's residents mostly welcomed this influx with a generosity of spirit, providing support for refugees as well as those relocating with new employers. Indeed, a specific Belgian Hospitality Fund was set up. Publicity in town reflected its diverse population with advertisements and public notices published in English, French and Flemish.

75 German Zeppelins over Letchworth

could not destroy our firmly established reputation for supplying the best possible value for money.

All

working parties now realise that our selection of Flannels, Flannelettes, Calicoes, etc., is the most varied and therefore the best, especially as the price is

Brought Down

as low as possible to meet with everybody's satisfaction

E. H. WIGHTMAN

Letchworth's population growth during the war years put even more pressure on housing and the need for more accommodation became acute. Owing to the restrictions on building, overcrowding was a real problem and even though some additional cottages were built during the war (on Spring Road by Howard Cottages) these were not enough to relieve supply problems. Letchworth was granted an exception to the national stop on building because of the demand for houses from Belgians and other factory workers. By this time the town was not alone and nationally the shortage in housing supply was quoted as being around 500,000 units. Despite this shortage and problems of overcrowding, Letchworth remained a healthy town.

Certainly, productivity in the town suffered, given the loss of men to service. A list published in *The Citizen* in September 1914 shows the impact across employers in the town. By September, over 200 men had enlisted or joined up and by January 1916 that number was around 800 men. A report by First Garden City Ltd states *"At first the outbreak of war caused a serious dislocation of the industries of the town, but there was little or nothing in the nature of panic. The place pulled itself together remarkably well"*. It goes on to commend the efforts of *"the chamber of commerce on the lines of maintaining business as usual"*.

Letchworth certainly did its bit during the war and a number of manufacturers were engaged in work for government, providing munitions, and more besides. A plant for processing coal tar, by which is produced toluol, a constituent of high explosives, was also added to the gas works at the request of the government.

With so many men away at war there were new employment opportunities for women, though the character of industries in town already ensured availability of work for them (e.g., weaving, embroidery, corsetry and printing). Firms actively sought women for the heavy industrial work that was once considered the preserve of men. They even offered comparable pay. An advertisement in *The Citizen* seeks women aged between seventeen and twenty years for *"machining aircraft parts and fittings and manufacture of time fuses"*. Many women became nurses: VADs – Voluntary Aid Detachment and Red Cross Nurses. Letchworth's Women's Reserve was formed, a movement aimed at organising the women's roles.

The Citizen kept townsfolk abreast of war news, including publishing regular letters from soldiers, reports of the wounded or those tragically lost as the war went on. There were also many good news stories, such as a party held at the new Spirella factory for Letchworth's 401 soldiers' families and thank you letters from troops to Spirella for the *"fine body belt sent to every Letchworth soldier"*.

People were encouraged to do their bit by making the most of their garden and early on Ebenezer Howard wrote to residents giving advice and tips. There were even wartime cookery demonstrations for suet puddings and toad in the hole, which were very well attended. Boy Scouts were engaged in egg collecting to nourish wounded soldiers – part of a national campaign for 200,000 freshly laid eggs a week.

By 1916 all possible areas, even to the centre of town, were devoted to growing food and areas intended for building were being used for agricultural purposes. But despite these efforts a shortage of horses and increased cost and scarcity of manual labour had a negative impact on agricultural productivity in the garden city.

Residents in Letchworth enjoyed a diverse choice of retailers in the town and many made light of the war in their efforts to boost sales. Interestingly, there did not seem to be the significant shortage of goods experienced during the Second World War, with many shops managing to source alternatives and other British-made goods. There was a brief period of panic buying on the outbreak of war but this soon disappeared.

Social life was important; clubs continued to flourish, theatrical life was vigorous (plays by Tolstoy, Hardy, Shakespeare, Shaw and Galsworthy were all performed); Garden City Pantomimes became well established in Howard Hall. The Picture Palace cinema advertised regular shows and boasted a different programme every night. There was also the Golf Club (although its membership and income suffered during the war), the swimming bath, bowling greens and athletic clubs of all kinds. Letchworth's Museum in the town square managed to open in 1914.

HOMESGARTH,
LETCHWORTH.

August 10th, 1914.

DEAR BROTHERS AND SISTERS,

The war has already raised the price of food, and prices may yet further advance—even after the war comes to an end, and that may be yet a long, long way off.

Now, your garden will help you very greatly in this trying time, if only you set to work AT ONCE.

One-tenth of an acre (or, say, 140 feet by 30 feet) will, if diligently cultivated, produce vegetables for *a family of four*.

If you do not know how to proceed, go at once to the nearest gentleman named on the next page—all friends of mine—who will give advice freely and gladly. They have also a small fund at their disposal for seeds, etc., but do not draw on this fund unless your need is urgent.

Yours very truly,

EBENEZER HOWARD.

The War and Your Garden –
letter to Letchworth residents
from Ebenezer Howard, 10th
August 1914.

NORTH OF RAILWAY.

EAST OF NORTON WAY.

R. MAHER, 6. Common View.
R. GARROD, 126, Common View.
F. COLLINS, 39, Common View.
W. J. THOMPSON, 119, Common View.
G. NEWMAN, " Muirloe Cottage," Norton Road.
F. ARNOTT, " The Briars," 9, Temple Gardens.
H. J. PHILLIPS, " Grasmere," 10, Temple Gardens.

WEST OF NORTON WAY.

HAL JONES, " Norton Croft," Wilbury Road.
G. W. WAUGH, " Sunnydene," Norton Way N.
H. HERRINGTON, 1, Cross St., corner Icknield Way.
W. J. TRUMAN, " Quita," 228, Nevells Road.

SOUTH OF RAILWAY.

EAST OF NORTON WAY.

T. H. JERMYN & E. PERRY, " Milton," 185, Baldock Road.
R. L. SHOEBRIDGE, 171, Baldock Road.
E. BRIDGES, 59, Ridge Road.
G. A. BOND, 67, Ridge Road.
H. BRIARS, 25, Ridge Avenue.
A. G. SCOTT, 4, Pix Road.
E. W. MARCH, 45, Pix Road.

WEST OF NORTON WAY.

J. CORBY, " Alpha Cottages," Baldock Road.
T. NEWELL, the Gardener at " Homesgarth," Sollershott.
E. J. HILL, " Coleacre," Barrington Road, Baldock Rd.
E. GATTRELL, Gardener to Mr. H. D. Pearsall, Garth Road, Baldock Road.
W. CLUNIE, 349, Norton Way.
J. SPICER, 34, Lytton Avenue.
T. H. CLACK, 24, Lytton Avenue.

A FEW HINTS.

The following hints are offered by an expert committee called for the purpose :

In a general way the average Letchworth garden ground should not be deeply dug at this season. A gentle easing of the top two or three inches of soil, and cleansing with a hoe, produce a bed more conducive to quick germination of seed (a very desirable condition with the shortening season of growth) than where the ground is recently and deeply dug.

Ground that has been used for early potatoes should be made moderately firm before sowing or planting.

It is not too late to plant—not to sow—good-sized plants of Savoy, Kale, Purple and White Broccoli, and Leeks.

Turnip seed (Red Globe and Green Globe) can be sown in full confidence.

Early Horn Carrot has a good chance.

The carrot requires better soil than turnips, but not recently manured.

Sow Winter Spinach (on rich soil only).

Onions are a profitable crop, and should be sown now (Tripoli varieties, Giant Rocca, Ailsa Craig).

Sow immediately Spring Cabbage seed (Early Offenham, Enfield Market, Ellam's Early, Wheeler's Imperial).

CONCLUSIONS

Modern day aerial photograph, Letchworth Garden City 2013. © Letchworth Garden City Heritage Foundation.

The challenge for today's garden cities

The garden city model is once again being used as a solution but this time to tackle a different problem, primarily addressing the acute shortage of housing across the country, but still taking the basic concept of starting afresh and creating new communities in a properly planned way. The new garden cities are being led by public, not private, development corporations, providing oversight and acting as enablers in a role not dissimilar to that of FGC Ltd.

With the passage of time and modern interpretations of garden cities, it is easy to forget how central industry was as a rich source of sustainable employment for a new town. Attracting industry underpinned many of the considerations about how Letchworth was planned and developed. (The 2011 Census found that 42 per cent of the population of Letchworth worked in North Hertfordshire, primarily in manufacturing.) Balancing the residential and industrial aspects was also really important. The town needed to be attractive to a wide range of potential residents, investors and businesses, outside the manufacturing and industrial aspects. Today there is concern that the demarcation between the industrial and residential areas is being eroded as former industrial brownfield sites are being developed as housing.

Providing a pleasant environment was critical in being able to fulfil promises of a better life at Letchworth. This meant conserving and enhancing the natural features of the estate wherever possible and ensuring that development was carefully managed and well designed (whether residential, factories or workshops) to provide better living and working conditions. Letchworth had to look and feel very different from other industrial towns. This characteristic was used as part of Company marketing with slogans like *"No Place Like Letchworth"*; at that time Letchworth offered modern, well designed and well sited industrial premises, idyllic residential areas and plenty of amenities for residents and visitors alike. To qualify as a garden city, it had to be self-sustaining and combine the benefits of country and town.

It remains to be seen the extent to which our modern garden cities measure up to these Letchworth credentials but it is hard to see how they can possibly deliver the quality of living environment with such significantly different housing densities, land constraints and overall development costs which will have a bearing on design and layout. Land costs alone are significant – in summer 2017, Knight Frank estate agents wrote of rising values of good quality arable land in southern and central England; up to £10,000 per acre had been realised in recent sales. This is more than double the equivalent uprated cost per acre of the land FGC Ltd purchased for Letchworth in 1903.

These days the chances of being able to find, afford and completely purchase a ring fence of virgin land big enough to develop a new town is unlikely, so today's garden cities will need to work with multiple landowners and a planning regime that can sometimes hinder development. The time taken from developing the master plan for Letchworth to undertaking first works on the estate was under six months. This would be totally impossible today.

Delivering such an ambitious garden city scheme at Letchworth required significant and sustained effort on the part of the Company's directors, shareholders and wider supporters. Private investment delivered key infrastructure and enabled development. Today it is the public sector which is supporting infrastructure and unlocking private-sector development of key sites for housing, employment and leisure. Letchworth was a wholly commercial venture geared towards public good and its progress was under the control of one company which was also the landowner. The fact that 31 per cent of Letchworth's residents (as recorded by the 2011 Census) occupy social housing is a legacy of the house-building undertaken by First Garden City Ltd (Letchworth Cottages & Buildings Ltd) and the various cottage societies of the early twentieth century, together with the building of the large estates at the Grange and Jackmans some 40–50 years later. Today public-sector bodies enable delivery across areas identified for new garden cities, which are often in (and will remain in) multiple ownership.

It is impossible to say how Letchworth would have developed if the First World War had not happened, but any shortcomings in the present-day town are not the fault of the garden city model. Howard himself recognised that the different social classes never really mixed, either residentially or socially, something which pertains today. In his second garden city at Welwyn, there was a clearer division of areas of housing and manufacture, bisected by the railway line. Welwyn Garden City was begun in 1920, the date when this book ends and when British society was starting to change in all sorts of ways; it differs from Letchworth in having a different governance model and being much more of a commuter town. The challenge for any twenty-first century garden city is to remain faithful to the housing and employment model conceived by Howard and his colleagues.

Against this backdrop, Letchworth Garden City is truly unique as the world's first garden city. It remains a beautiful and diverse town today, standing as a testament to its founders and as a legacy for future residents.

AFTERWORD

Sollershott Hall, c. 1910, photographed by Arthur Clutterbuck. Reproduced by kind permission of Kim Fisher.

LEARNING FROM LETCHWORTH GARDEN CITY

Anne Coste, Stéphane Sadoux, Susannah O'Carroll, Centre of Excellence in Architecture, Environment & Building Cultures, Grenoble School of Architecture, Université Grenoble Alpes

A few years ago we decided to put garden cities at the heart of our research, not least because we believe that, as precedents, they are particularly interesting to study in the context of current issues relating to housing, health, and the environment. The "GC21 – Garden Cities for the 21st Century" project was launched by the Centre of Excellence in Architecture, Environment & Building Cultures (LabEx Architecture, Environnement & Cultures Constructives) in 2014. It focuses on the past, present and future of garden cities and involves a number of researchers, PhD candidates and postdoctoral students.

As researchers at the Centre of Excellence in Architecture, Environment & Building Cultures (Université Grenoble Alpes), we study the history of architecture and urbanism in the light of today's environmental, social, economic and public health crises. Garden cities are, from our point of view, worth examining from two perspectives: first as a theory, based on the writings of Ebenezer Howard; second, as experiments in Letchworth and Welwyn. As historians, we believe that research into garden cities should be carried out in a way that allows us to understand better current concerns. As University teachers, we are convinced that garden cities offer students a robust model which can help them think about the complexity of architectural and urban design in the light of current economic, social, public health and housing crises. Although the context Howard worked in was, of course, very different, the approach he developed, which aimed to address multiple and simultaneous crises, is worth reflecting upon.

Learning from a systemic approach

Like our friends in the Letchworth Local History Research Group, we believe that one of the main strengths of the garden city theory is that the new type of human settlement it suggested was designed as a social, economic, political and ecological system. Industry, of course, was an integral part of this complex system. Letchworth, the first practical experiment based on this theory, was designed as an industrial town, in which industry was considered in terms of production, but also in the light of its social and urban dimensions and its relation to the environment. This approach was also underpinned by a concern for the wellbeing of populations:

> *The idea [of the founders] that it is equally necessary that factories and workshops should be taken out of crowded towns and be healthy and pleasant places, conducted under modern conditions, and not too far from the workmen's homes, or too far from un-built-on land, and to add further proof to that given by Bournville, and other factories, that this is not only an ideal to be desired but is 'good business'." (What does Garden City Stand for? the Letchworth Branch of the Garden City Association (Residents' Union), c.1910, Letchworth: Garden City Collection LBM3056.33.23)*

Regardless of garden cities' architectural and urban qualities, to look at them merely from a physical point of view is somewhat to miss the point. Their architects did not only draw up master plans: they adopted a comprehensive approach and thought about ways of dealing with economic development and industries. A number of architectural historians have misunderstood this. As an illustration, Curtis has claimed that

> *"Essentially [Howard's] vision of local communities was a variant on the English village, but with additional amenities like railways and small-scale industry. The unit in the Garden City was the family in its individual home; these houses were to be laid out along well-planted streets, converging gradually upon the broad communal green and civic buildings towards the centre." (Curtis, 982).*

This gradual distortion of the original model, which is evident in the post-war British new towns, is also apparent in a number of so-called garden settlements, which are currently being built throughout the country. The Town and Country Planning Association stressed that Garden City principles are indivisible and interlocking, and expressed concerns that new garden cities, such as Ebbsfleet, ignore these principles (Mark, 2014).

Only Letchworth still boasts the original features of a garden city. This book shows that in the first garden city industry is still as important as it was when the settlement was founded.

Both an Industrial City and the City of Health

One aspect of our research focuses on the place of health in urbanism. As the world faces the Covid-19 health crisis, it seems that Howard's work is more relevant than ever. Of particular interest is one of his manuscripts, dated 1890-91 and titled *City of Health and how to build it*, which is now held in the Hertfordshire Archives and Local Studies. It shows that he thought about industry from the start:

> *The first and essential question would be a site. [...] Then is it not the fact that certain trades and manufactures have their natural centres and would it be possible to transfer sufficient trades in anything like a wholesale manner to such a site? (City of Health and how to build it, p16)*

Howard also linked this to local resources. He describes materials, their transport and processing:

> *My Board have an excellent one [site] of 5 acres, within a mile of a railway station. There is at present no approach but work on the site will be at once commenced. There is an excellent brickfield within one mile and a road leading from it with a kiln. A temporary tramway will also be put in hand forthwith when bricks will be delivered at any part of the site at the moderate price of [blank] per thousand. There is also excellent stone on the Company's estate which will be supplied at moderate rates, as, of course there will be no railway or canals to pay" (Ibid. p. 29)*

The same text shows that Howard had thought about the contribution of industry to the garden city's socio-economic model in the early 1890s. He aimed not only to encourage development and offer jobs, but also to provide a fund which would be used for the benefit of the community:

> *Another possible advantage we can offer you is this. You will see by the Plan it is proposed to erect markets in the town. The entire profits from these and from other works in which the Company at present and the City in time to come will be engaged and from the rents derived from the occupiers of factories will, after paying the interest on the debentures and the expense of management, be entirely devoted to City improvements, and, when the city is in a position to do so it will doubtless arrange to make contributions to the funds of your Society, as also of the other Institutions of a [related] nature, which it is hoped will make the town one of special attractiveness to all those who have the interests of a community at heart. (Ibid. p. 31)*

This system is based on a mutually profitable approach and always provides compensation: the industry contributes to the community's well-being, since it attracts and retains a workforce whose living conditions are far better than they would be in overpopulated cities.

Howard produced diagrams rather than master plans. These diagrams, nevertheless, suggested a theoretical spatial layout, in which factories are strategically linked to infrastructure, for example, train lines, stations, tramways, and to training institutions as well as retail spaces. Factories are located on the fringe of the garden city and are therefore connected to working-class and middle-class housing, but also to road and rail networks. An essential component of this system is framed by a control of urban growth: the central garden city's population should not exceed 50,000 inhabitants, whilst other satellites are limited to 32,000. The network can thus function, whilst pollution and costs are limited.

We now come to the outer ring. There are the factories and coach houses, the dairies, markets and technical schools [map reference] which last have thus the almost unique advantage of being close to the industries taught [,] involving an enormous economy in regard to appliances. The railway station is at [map reference – but all around that] and a circular railway encompassing the whole city with siding accommodation enables goods to be loaded direct into trucks from warehouses and workshops or to be taken direct from the trucks into the warehouses or factories. The readiness with which a train load can be got up will be at once imagined. (Ibid. p. 12-13)

Our research involved a study of the Cheap Cottages Exhibition (1905) and of the Urban Housing and Rural Homesteads Exhibition (1907). The 'Population Growth and Demand for Housing' section of this book shows how these were linked to the development of industry. The history of cheap cottages throws light on contemporary political and social issues, and on the experimental dimension of Letchworth as regards working-class housing. One other experiment, however, is worth mentioning: Sollershott Hall, a co-operative housing block, was built in 1909. According to Tony Parker (2002), the project aimed at addressing the 'servant problem' and provided single professional people with amenities such as heating, lighting, cleaning and laundry facilities. Meals were cooked in the communal kitchen and residents could either eat together in the dining room or have their meals delivered to their homes. Parker also explains that after the Second World War, servants were replaced by staff who worked in local factories.

The project was initiated by Letchworth Co-Operative Houses Limited, a not-for-profit company of which Ebenezer Howard was one of the directors. The project was funded by investors, whose interest in the venture was encouraged by extensive press coverage. Several types of homes were on offer: one, two or three bedrooms with private or shared bathroom. The complex included shared spaces and gardens. This successful precedent could provide a valuable source of inspiration for today's designers.

Sollershott Hall's architectural design reflects garden city principles and the idea of sharing. The first phase of the development comprised L-shaped buildings which were laid out around a large green space and an orchard. The buildings erected during the second phase completed the rectangle and the development is similar to what would nowadays be referred to as an open block. The heart of the block is a space which is maintained and used by the residents of Sollershott Hall, but is also accessible to people from the neighbourhood. The housing units are finely designed brick buildings, with brick frontages on the ground floor, white rendering on the first floor and a slate pitched roof. Amenities such as a laundry room and the heating system are grouped together and located in taller buildings, in a wing that used to accommodate the kitchen, the dining room and leisure spaces. Car parks, bicycle sheds and bin stores are located at the back of the buildings, accessible from the street.

*Sollershott Hall,
Letchworth Garden
City. Photographs:
A. Coste, 2017*

Letchworth Garden City: a common good and a model

The authors of this book, who live in the garden city, love the place they live in. They adopted a scientific approach to document, study and promote it. As academics, we decided to research the garden city and also fell in love with it. It is therefore not surprising that our paths crossed. The research group wrote this book for the residents of Letchworth and the general public. We are delighted and honoured to have been invited to contribute to it, for two reasons. First, because it gives us an opportunity to thank the research group for their warm welcome and generosity during our field work in Letchworth, and for sharing invaluable information about the garden city, its history and architecture. We are most grateful for the time Janet and Philippa spent with us, to answer our questions, invite us inside their homes and take us around Industrial Letchworth. We have fond memories of our trips to Hertfordshire: walking around garden cities, experiencing the local life, studying in the archives and discovering Howard's handwritten papers, and being mesmerised by some architectural features which are documented in this volume. The second reason is that we carry out our research in partnership with local stakeholders, not only because of their knowledge, but also because we believe it is important to design research questions with them. Working in Hertfordshire was very rewarding and enriching: we collaborated with the University of Hertfordshire, Hertfordshire Archives and Local Studies, the Garden City Collection, the International Garden Cities Institute, Letchworth Garden City Heritage Foundation and the Welwyn Garden City Heritage Trust. They all contribute to local knowledge and also to international outreach. These individuals and groups contributed to strengthening our own knowledge, which we share with our students, so garden cities continue to provide an inspiration for today and tomorrow.

We also express our gratitude to Lord Salisbury, whose passion for traditional architecture and urbanism, and support for our research have been invaluable.

BIBLIOGRAPHY AND SOURCES

Printed books

Agar, Nigel, *Behind the Plough: Agrarian Society in Nineteenth-Century Hertfordshire*.
(Hatfield: University of Hertfordshire Press, 2005)

Armytage, W H G, *Heavens Below: Utopian Experiments in England 1560–1960*.
(London: Routledge and Kegan Paul, 1961)

Beevers, Robert, *The Garden City Utopia: A Critical Biography of Ebenezer Howard*. (London:
Macmillan, 1988)

Buder, Stanley, *Visionaries and Planners: The Garden City Movement and The Modern Community*.
(Oxford: OUP, 1990)

Christie-Miller, Geoffrey, Collier, Gerrard and Howarth, Edward, *Report of a Temporary Colony
at Garden City for Unemployed Workmen Mainly from West Ham During February, March and April
1905*. (London: P S King & Son, 1905)

Curtis, William J. R. *Modern Architecture since 1900* (London: Phaidon, 1982)

Fishman, Robert, *Urban Utopias in the Twentieth Century: Ebenezer Howard, Frank Lloyd Wright and
Le Corbusier*. (Cambridge, MA: MIT Press, 1982)

Garden City Collection, *Letchworth Garden City Food Tour: A Guide to Butchers, Bakers & Vegetarian
Sausage Makers in the Early Garden City*. (Letchworth Garden City Heritage Foundation, nd
c.2016)

Hamnett, Chris & Randolph, Bill, *Cities, Housing and Profits: Flat Break Up and the Decline of
Private Renting*. (London: Hutchinson, 1988)

Hardy, Dennis, *Utopian England – Community Experiments 1900–1945*.
(London: E & F N Spon, 2000)

Howard, Ebenezer, *Garden Cities of To-Morrow*.
Edited with a preface by F J Osborn (Cambridge, Mass: MIT Press, 1965)
A later version of Howard's *To-morrow: A Peaceful Path to Real Reform* (1898)

Letchworth Urban District Council, *Coronation Booklet – A Pageant of Letchworth History 1937*
(Letchworth: St Christopher Press & Garden City Press, 1937)

Meacham, Standish, *Regaining Paradise: Englishness and the Early Garden City Movement*.
(New Haven and London: Yale University Press, 1999)

Miller, Mervyn, *Letchworth: The First Garden City*.
Second edition (Chichester: Phillimore, 2002)

National Library Week Committee, *Letchworth: A Town Built on a Book*. (Letchworth, 1966)

Parker, Tony, *A brief history of Sollershott Hall: Booklet prepared for the owners and residents of
Sollershott Hall* [2002]

Purdom, C B, *The Garden City: A Study in the Development of a Modern Town*.
(London: J. M. Dent, 1913)

Purdom, C B, *The Building of Satellite Towns: A Contribution to the Study of Town Development and Regional Planning.* New edition (London: J. M. Dent, 1949)

Simpson, Michael, *Thomas Adams and the Modern Planning Movement: Britain, Canada and the United States, 1900–1940.* (London: Mansell Publishing, 1985)

Ward, Stephen V, *The Peaceful Path: Building Garden Cities and New Towns.* (Hatfield: University of Hertfordshire Press, 2016)

Periodicals and journals

Garden City Association Journals:

* *The Garden City*
* *Garden Cities and Town Planning Magazine*

Garden City Press [Hitchin] newspaper 1904

Old Motor and Vintage Commercial January 1964

Motoring and Leisure magazine, Article: "Made in Herts", October 1986

Spirella Magazine, published monthly by The Spirella Company of Great Britain Ltd, Letchworth (Garden City), Herts. Later "Threads", House Journal of Spirella

The Automobile Vol. 3 No. 9, November 1985

The Aeroplane Vol. 18, 1920

The Citizen [Letchworth] newspaper 1907–1920

"Sollershott Hall: report of a talk given to Letchworth Garden City Society". In *The Letchworth Garden City Society Journal*, No. 149, September 2017, pp. 3–5

Mark, Laura "Ebbsfleet plans ignore garden city principles, says concerned TCPA". In *Architects' Journal* 12 August 2014.

The Surveyor and Municipal and County Engineer, "Garden Cities, A Method of Industrial Distribution", by Ralph Neville KC., 5 February 1904

Vernet, Nicolas and Coste, Anne "Garden Cities of the 21st Century: A Sustainable Path to Suburban Reform". In *Urban Planning* 2 (4) 2017, pp. 45–60.

Archives

Hertfordshire Archives and Local Studies, Hertford

* "Guide to Garden City", (The Garden City Press, c.1905)
* First Garden City Ltd, "Prospectus" (Furnival Press, 8 September 1903)
* First Garden City Ltd, "Directors' Report" (May 1904) and Appendix to Report "System of Land Tenure" (April 1904)
* Pamphlet – "First Garden City Ltd – The first practical outcome of the Garden City Association"
* Thomas Adams, First Garden City Ltd, "The First Garden City, Notes on plan of proposed town" (April 1904)
* Barry Parker and Raymond Unwin, "First Garden City, Plan of Estate and Proposed Town" (c. April 1904)

- Barry Parker and Raymond Unwin, "Garden City Estate, Plan of Proposed Town" (c. April1904)
- Plan "Garden City Estate" (accompanies plan listed above, also prepared by Parker and Unwin)
- Plan "Garden City as it will be"
- Pamphlet – "How to See (Letchworth Garden City) May 1906" (Letchworth: Garden City Press Ltd, 1906)
- Residents' Survey, Letchworth Garden City (c.1908/1909)
- City of Health and how to build it. Carbon copy pages of lecture or article [pages 1-32, page 22 missing] with marginalia, nd [c. 1890 – 1891]

The Garden City Collection, Letchworth Garden City

- First Garden City Ltd, Balance Sheet and Schedules (1904–1921)
- Garden City Pioneer Company Ltd, – Miscellaneous Company correspondence (1902–1903)
- First Garden City Ltd, – Miscellaneous Company correspondence, (1903–1920)
- First Garden City Ltd, Directors' Reports (1904–1920)
- First Garden City Ltd, – Plot Files (various)
- Pamphlet – First Garden City Ltd, "Why Manufacturers Should Move to Letchworth" (various editions)
- Pamphlet – First Garden City Ltd, "The Only New Industrial Town in England" (1913 and 1915)
- Pamphlet – First Garden City Ltd, "Opening of the Gas Works, October 10, 1905"
- Pamphlet – First Garden City Ltd, "Letchworth (Garden City) Press View" (20 August 1908)
- Pamphlet – First Garden City Ltd, "A Visit to Letchworth (Garden City)" (27 July 1907)
- Pamphlet – First Garden City Ltd, "A Few Queries about Garden City, The Question and the Answer, September 1911" (Letchworth:Garden City Press Ltd, 1911)
- Pamphlet – First Garden City Ltd, "Letchworth Garden City, Visit of the Employees of J. M. Dent & Co"
- Pamphlet – "Garden City in the Making" (Letchworth:Garden City Press Ltd, 1905)
- Pamphlet – "Furniture Made by Woodworkers Ltd at Letchworth" (Letchworth: Arden Press, c.1913)
- Pamphlet – "A Note on Garden City, Light on Housing and Industrial Problems" (Letchworth: Garden City Press, nd.)
- Pamphlet – Prospectus (Letchworth: Garden City Press Ltd,1903–06)

Letchworth Garden City Library, Letchworth

- Letchworth Directories (1905–1920)

Warner Textile Archive, Braintree, Essex:

- Archive materials relating to the St Edmundsbury Weaving Works, Letchworth

British Newspaper Archive

- Various press articles on the Garden City Association, Garden City Pioneer Company and First Garden City Ltd, regarding the garden city, 1901–1905, www.britishnewspaperarchive.co.uk

Online sources

Database: Letchworth Local History Group 1911 Census research (unpublished)

The Co-operatives Heritage Trust – www.co-operativeheritage.coop

Grace's Guide to British Industrial History (Lacre, Phoenix, Kryn & Lahy and Heatly Gresham) – www.gracesguide.co.uk

St. Edmundsbury Designs – www.edmundsbury.co.uk

Wikipedia – www.wikipedia.org